Our Bible Too

Our Bible Too

A New Soteriology of Messianic Judaism

JEFFREY W. DANDOY

WIPF & STOCK · Eugene, Oregon

OUR BIBLE TOO
A New Soteriology of Messianic Judaism

Copyright © 2021 Jeffrey W. Dandoy. All rights reserved. Except for brief quotations in critical publications or reviews, no part of this book may be reproduced in any manner without prior written permission from the publisher. Write: Permissions, Wipf and Stock Publishers, 199 W. 8th Ave., Suite 3, Eugene, OR 97401.

Wipf & Stock
An Imprint of Wipf and Stock Publishers
199 W. 8th Ave., Suite 3
Eugene, OR 97401

www.wipfandstock.com

PAPERBACK ISBN: 978-1-7252-9996-2
HARDCOVER ISBN: 978-1-7252-9997-9
EBOOK ISBN: 978-1-7252-9998-6

03/31/21

Dedicated to the Messianic congregations of Beit HaTorah and Rosh Pina for their worship, fellowship, and nurture.

"A keen single force draws our yearning
for the utmost out of the seclusion of the soul.
We try to see our visions in His light,
to feel our life as His affair."

Abraham Joshua Heschel[1]

---

1. Heschel, "Prayer," 353.

Contents

Permissions		ix
Acknowledgments		xi
Introduction		xiii
1	Newer than New	1
2	Airing Our Linen	13
Discussion A: When the Old Testament Isn't Old		24
3	The Messianic Heavenly Vision	27
4	A Way Through the Muddle	37
5	The Jewish Soul and the Holy Spirit	48
Discussion B: Believing as Gentiles and as Jews		57
6	Commentary on Romans 9, 10, and 11	61
7	Three Men at a Train Station	97
Discussion C: A Place for Jews in God's Plan and Purpose for this World		106
8	Correspondence with Rabbi Adam Yisroel	110
9	Beyond Complaint	118
Discussion D: Judaism as Seen Through Christian Eyes		127
10	Different Assumptions: Different Religion	131
11	The Bible Without Old and New Testaments	141
12	Renewed Fear	150
Conclusion		160
Bibliography		167
Index of Names		171
Index of Subjects		173
Index of Scripture		177

Permissions

All Scripture quotations, unless otherwise indicated, are taken from The Holy Bible, *New International Version, NIV*. Copyright 1973, 1978, 1984, 2011 by Biblica, Inc. Used by permission. All rights reserved worldwide.

Scripture quotations marked NASB are taken from the *New American Standard Bible*. Copyright 1906, 1962, 1963, 1968, 1971, 1972, 1973, 1975, 1977, 1995 by The Lockman Foundation. Used by permission.

The Scripture quotations marked NRSV are from the *New Revised Standard Version of the Bible*. Copyright 1989 by the Division of Christian Education of the National Council of Churches of Christ in the United States of America, and are used by permission. All rights reserved.

Scripture quotations marked RSV are taken from the *Revised Standard Version of the Bible*. Copyright 1946, 1952, 1971 by the Division of Christian Education of the National Council of Churches of Christ in the USA. Used by permission.

Scripture quotation marked OJB is taken from *The Orthodox Jewish Bible*. Copyright 2011 by AFI International. All rights reserved.

Scripture quotations marked as KJV are taken from the King James Version.

Quotation from *Catch the Jew!* by Tuvia Tenenbom (New York: Gefen Publishing House Ltd., 2015) is used by permission.

Quotations from *Deliverance to the Captives* by Karl Barth. Translated by Marguerite Wieser. Copyright 1961, 1989 by SCM Press, Ltd. Used by permission of HarperCollins Publishers.

Permissions

Quotation from *Misquoting Jesus* by Bart D. Ehrman. Copyright 2005 by Bart D. Ehrman. Used by permission of HarperCollins Publishers.

Quotation from *The Words of Gardner Taylor, Volume 1: NBC Radio Sermons, 1959–1970* by Gardner C. Taylor, ed. by Edward L. Taylor (Valley Forge: Judson Press, 1999) is used by permission.

Quotations from *Mapping Messianic Jewish Theology: A Constructive Approach* by Richard Harvey. Copyright 2009 by Richard Harvey. Published by Paternoster. Reproduced with permission of the Licensor through PLSclear.

Quotations from "Messianic Jews Debate the Deity of Jesus" by Aviel Schneider are used by permission of *Israel Today*.

Quotations from *Basic Judaism* by Milton Steinberg. Copyright 1947 by Milton Steinberg, renewed 1974 by David Joel Steinberg and Jonathan Steinberg. Used by permission of Houghton Mifflin Harcourt Publishing Company. All rights reserved.

Quotations from *Messianic Judaism* by Carol Harris-Shapiro (1999). Reprinted by permission of Beacon Press, Boston.

Quotations from Between Cross and Crescent: Jewish Civilization from Mohammed to Spinoza. Copyright 2005 The Teaching Company. LLC. Reproduced with permission of The Teaching Company, LLC, www.thegreatcourses.com

Acknowledgments

My wife Lesley was my first reader and an indefatigable support over the years it took for the vision to reach its fulfillment. Her patience and love were key contributions. I wish to acknowledge as well the timely intervention I received from Joya Stevenson, whose encouragement and instruction elevated my determination and vision to see the work through to its completion. Her developmental editing cast a light of improvement for the project. The book would also not have been possible without the faith Wipf and Stock Publishers had in a first-time author. Credit for getting this book into your hands goes to them.

Introduction

A New Idea

If you are unversed in Christianity, Judaism, or Messianic Judaism, the questions and answers in these pages may seem small as you begin. Hopefully not by the time you finish. To an outsider the differences in the religions that use the Bible are dwarfed by their fantastic belief that the Bible is an authority for life sent as a revelation from God. On the near side of that leap of faith and logic, everyone on the far side looks pretty much the same: religious.

Welcome to the far side. Here the differences matter a great deal. As the unversed reader contemplates them it may occur to her that God is real, God did inspire the Bible and perhaps God even inspired her to pick up this book to read—because the inspiration and revelation of God is not just between the covers of the Bible. It is a dynamic process at work in people today.

Messianic Jews are experiencing God in their midst, setting them apart for a new and holy purpose. The God of the Bible is showing up in a new way that is neither Christianity nor Judaism. Yet all of us can learn from, and be challenged by, God's new idea.

I discovered this for myself in a powerful way at the age of forty-five when, having all my life only known God through the Christian faith, he revealed himself to me anew through Messianic Judaism. It was as sudden as it was unexpected and inconvenient. The truth of my existence flipped.

If God was doing a new thing wouldn't you want to know about it? Working through the revelation in Messianic Judaism was the occasion for examining the assumptions in the orthodoxies of the faiths from which it arose. What do Christians assume? What do Jews assume? How did Messianic Judaism arrive with a new set of assumptions?

Messianic Judaism works, but in conventional thought it should not. It is either a sect in Christianity or a blasphemy in Judaism. Both are assertions of false religion. But instead Messianic Judaism is a true religion. Richard Harvey explains:

> Messianic Judaism is the religion of Jewish people who believe in Jesus (Yeshua) as the promised Messiah. It is a Jewish form of Christianity and a Christian form of Judaism, challenging the boundaries and beliefs of both.[2]

Messianic Rabbi Mark Kinzer and most members of Messianic congregations are not really concerned about apparent contradictions. Their experience of God lifts them above criticism of skeptics. Kinzer writes, "The fundamental reality we must be concerned with is not that of theological propositions, but instead the worship practices that express and shape our actual relationship with God."[3]

Adding Testament to Testaments

Still, orthodoxy ("right worship") must make sense to avoid becoming nonsense. To inspire, to instruct, and ultimately to save, our teaching must shine divine light into our souls and minds. Soteriology is the study of salvation. It is a Greek/Western/ecclesiastical discipline that grew out of disputes among the early church fathers, although the first known use of the word was circa 1774.[4] Christian soteriology focuses on God's act in Jesus Christ, which includes his incarnation, his atoning death, and his resurrection. The title given to the Christian scriptures, the new covenant or New Testament, captures the Christian claim of a new salvation from God.

Together with God's election, God's covenants with Israel are a basis for the salvation of Jews. Messianic Judaism is founded on both the new Christian testament and the prior Jewish testaments. A new soteriology of Messianic Judaism should be a scandal to the religious establishments of Christianity and Judaism, as it draws upon their own traditions to follow a new calling into the arms of God. An orthodoxy for this different religion still awaits a consensus.

---

2 Harvey, *Mapping Messianic Jewish Theology*, 1.

3 Kinzer, "Jewish Models," quoted in Harvey, *Mapping Messianic Jewish Theology*, 125.

4. *Merriam-Webster*, s.v. "soteriology," accessed November 30, 2020, www.merriam-webster.com/dictionary/.

Making Sense Monotheistically

As an evangelical in my formative years of faith, I embraced a doctrine of the Incarnation, "fully God and fully man," with no real difficulty—on the basis of faith and tradition of course, not on the basis of making logical sense. That is Christianity. That is the foundation for the church. But since God called me out of the church and out of Christianity, I am free to ask: "Really?" Because from the monotheistic perspective I have adopted, it does not register. From a rational perspective, it is nonsense. Was Jesus a stranger among us, a misfit like Superman? Was Jesus a miracle that was nonhuman, an alien to our species? Was this Jewish messiah, the anointed one, not really a man because he was hypostatic with dual natures?

If that is the Christian gospel can Messianic Jews now interpret the record monotheistically and proclaim him as a human being like everyone else who has ever lived? Can we follow this man who was chosen by God to initiate a new covenant through his life, death, and resurrection? We can by reading the New Testament with a monotheistic hermeneutic. Christians would not do that. But Jews could. Perhaps there is another truth now set loose in the world by the minority of Messianic Jews who insist on both one God and a revelation of that God in a fully and only human messiah.

Changing Roadmaps

The Jewish revelation of God as one (being non-trinitarian without a divine incarnation) is actually disputed within the Messianic Jewish movement. A minority rules out belief in a divine nature in Yeshua, and a majority holds to it. In Israel today the common sense of the word "Messianic" is as an adjective for Christian because of the belief in a divine messiah.[5] Around the world most Messianic congregations share the assumptions of the Protestant evangelical church without being Christians. The largest congregations, the most visible leadership, and the majority of Messianic Jews have adopted traditional Christian doctrine.[6] A representative example is the

---

5. Rudolph, "Messianic Judaism in Antiquity and in the Modern Era," 31–33.

6. McKee observes, "More frequent to be found among today's Messianic people, congregations, and various ministries and teachers of note would be some kind of principled high Christology." McKee, "Introducing the Divinity of Yeshua." Harvey notes, "The Creeds and Articles of Faith produced by Messianic Jewish organizations are uniformly orthodox from a Christian perspective;" and contrariwise, "Uri Marcus's position reflects the Arian and adoptionist Christologies of the early Church, and is influenced by the need to assert the singularity of God's oneness without compromise. This position, whilst attractive to some, remains a minority position." Harvey, *Mapping Messianic Jewish Theology*, 51, 138.

Union of Messianic Jewish Congregations (UMJC) that in 2005 published a statement to clarify their faith as one with the church:

> Jewish life is life in a concrete, historical community. Thus, Messianic Jewish groups must be fully part of the Jewish people, sharing its history and its covenantal responsibility as a people chosen by God. At the same time, faith in Yeshua also has a crucial communal dimension. This faith unites the Messianic Jewish community and the Christian Church, which is the assembly of the faithful from the nations who are joined to Israel through the Messiah. Together the Messianic Jewish community and the Christian Church constitute the *ekklesia*, the one Body of Messiah, a community of Jews and Gentiles who in their ongoing distinction and mutual blessing anticipate the shalom of the world to come.[7]

The inadequacy of this statement is its presumption to claim identity and belonging with the Jewish people and, "At the same time ... " claim identity and belonging with the Christian church. The apparent contradiction is real. It really does not make sense. And in fact, while being the roadmap of the majority, it has not led Messianic Judaism either into acceptance by the historic Jewish community as a branch of Judaism or into denominational, ecumenical standing in the church.[8]

I find the dual aspirations of the status quo—to be at the same time both outsiders and insiders—to be misguided. Our mission is not to reform the church or to renew Judaism. Our God is revealing to us a third way to read the Bible and be the people of God that is neither Christianity nor Judaism.

In the world of Messianic Judaism this is a minority opinion. While the title of this book, *Our Bible Too*, presumes to voice the claim of the Messianic Jewish movement, it is visionary. The community is not of one mind in its theology, its Christology, or its soteriology.[9] This vision is a way

---

7. Union of Messianic Jewish Congregations, "Defining Messianic Judaism."

8. Harris-Shapiro writes, "For those Jews accepting Jewish law as a standard of faith and practice it is clear that Messianic Judaism can hardly be called 'Judaism'. Accepting Jesus as Lord and Savior, while acceptable for the Gentiles as inculcating respect for God and the Bible, is clearly understood as a religion that abandons absolute monotheism and is thus off-limits to Jews .... This exclusion rankles Messianic Jews, who seek to have not only their status but also their legitimacy in the community affirmed." Harris-Shapiro, *Messianic Judaism*, 169–70.

9. McKee indicates, "For many, the Divinity of Yeshua ... is an essential Biblical truth. Given the diversity of theological beliefs in the broad Messianic movement, this is often *the issue* that people will divide over." McKee, "Introducing the Divinity of Yeshua"; Harvey observes, "Messianic Jewish thinkers have produced a series of theological

of achieving goals set forth by the majority: acceptance by the traditional Jewish establishment together with an appropriation of the New Testament that elevates us to equal standing with the church in a fellowship of belief. Not the same belief because it is not a vision of a kind of Christianity. Not the same religion as Judaism because it does not have not an identical soteriology. God is doing something new, and the old wineskins of Christianity and Judaism cannot contain it.

Maturing into Wisdom and Knowledge

In 2009, Richard Harvey lamented the lack of interest in the Messianic Jewish community in theological questions and answers:

> Whilst there is strong and heated debate on the subject, there is little *written* material on the doctrine of the Messiah, especially on the relationship between the Jewish understanding of the Messiah and the Christian understanding of God. Messianic Jews have yet to address the topic in an organized and reflective way, and there are several reasons for this.[10]

Harvey cites the lack of priority for doing systematic theology, in a movement that is busy growing congregations, as well as a lack of training in what has traditionally been a Christian discipline. He concludes with a word about the handicap of diversity among Messianic Jews:

> In addition, the Messianic movement has yet to develop the theological maturity to effectively speak on issues that have been the focus of controversy over many centuries. It is often divided on theological, cultural, geographical and generational lines, and there is no agreed mechanism or procedure for deciding key issues of theological orthodoxy. The presence of 'unorthodox views' is a matter of some embarrassment to leaders in the movement.[11]

Our Bible Too is the theological response of a Presbyterian minister called by God to leave the church for the truths and salvation of Messianic Judaism. It is an unorthodox response by the measure of most efforts by

---

and apologetic tracts that have come to define and defend the movement's path. In accordance with the relatively pluralistic nature of Messianic Judaism, their work has not been unified or uniform and has given voice to a large spectrum of opinions." Harvey, *Mapping Messianic Jewish Theology*, 32.

10. Harvey, *Mapping Messianic Jewish Theology*, 98.
11. Harvey, *Mapping Messianic Jewish Theology*, 98.

Messianic Jews to explain themselves. Where they have been unsuccessful, I offer a new definition of success: a religion with its own monotheistic way of interpreting the New Testament, grounded in faith in a human messiah and king—as all Jewish messiahs and kings have been. It is not Judaism, and that is okay. It is not Christianity, and that is okay. They are both okay in their ways, and we will be okay in ours as we trust in the wisdom and knowledge of God's new revelation: a third biblical religion claiming it is our Bible too.

People who trust in God, people who read and study the Bible, students of spirituality, of theology, of hermeneutics, of soteriology, of Judaism and of Christianity, are all addressed by the witness in these pages. It challenges common assumptions and easy answers. It is a new story of salvation that invites Jews and Christians into a new interfaith dialogue.

An Easy Format

Rabbi Eliezer Sneiderman is an Orthodox rabbi who taught at the University of Delaware in the town where I live. I attended his survey course on Jewish philosophy. When asked why he is often Socratic in his classroom instruction rather than simply lecturing from his treasury of knowledge he said the students are better equipped by learning to figure out things. I admire his restraint. If I know the answer, I will not patiently lead the uninitiated along by a series of questions until they realize it for themselves. I spill the beans.

So even though this book is divided into twelve chapters the reader can dive in anywhere and not be at a disadvantage. There are essays and sermons, there is biblical commentary and an exchange of letters, and there are four short lessons with questions for discussion. There is also mystery here, as in Yeshua's parable of The Seed Growing Secretly (Mark 4:26–29) in which the sower does not know how God's grace operates as it leads from the beginning to the end. Nevertheless, the beans are spilled all over. I sincerely appreciate having you as a reader. Be blessed.

Jeffrey W. Dandoy (Daniel)
May 29, 2020

1

Newer than New

Nothing in my background suggested I would leave the ministry and convert to Messianic Judaism. I studied Judaism in college where I read Chaim Potok's novel *The Chosen*. I visited Israel as the leader of my church group's tour of the Holy Land in 1995. But I was not thinking about making any change in my life when God spoke to me out of the blue in 2004 and put an urgency in my heart to go to the Messianic Jewish synagogue nearby. I did not leave Christianity out of disaffection. In fact I continued attending churches for years while also attending the synagogue. God opened a door and told me to walk through it. So I did.

Under Construction

From Rabbi Carol Harris-Shapiro in *Messianic Judaism: A Rabbi's Journey through Religious Change in America*:

> *The Challenge for the Messianic Movement*
> Adherents claim that Messianic Judaism resolved many contradictions in their lives and provided an answer to their prayers and problems. However, their proud assertions of authenticity coincided with some difficult contradictions. The conflicts Messianic believers face are not only with the American Jewish mainstream community and Christian churches, but also with the two contradictory cultural contexts—American Judaism

and Spirit-filled Protestantism—that shape the ever-present internal process of Messianic believers to construct and maintain a "new thing," Messianic Jewish identity.

Possibly what engenders the most conscious sense of tension among Messianic Jews is that they refuse to call their religious movement a "blend" of Judaism and Christianity. The self-appointed task of Messianic believers is to claim an ongoing *Jewish* identity, despite their belief in the divinity and saving power of Jesus of Nazareth. Herein lies the greatest struggle of all. As we will see, this identity claim is clearly contestable by both the Jewish and Christian communities, and thus the congregation continually works to re-create and re-establish this identity claim in sermons, music, dance, conversation, and even dress.[1]

The Messianic Jews I know are happy in their choice to claim both a Jewish identity and a belief in the saving power of Jesus. On the inside we get it. This confidence comes from a sense of calling. As Messianics we believe we are fulfilling God's will. Coming from God, it should all be a blessing. Instead, this blessing can become problematic.

This does not mean that Messianic Jews uncritically accept the definitions proffered by the American Jewish establishment. Messianic Jews want not merely to legitimate their perceived Jewish identity, but to *change* this identity. As "saved" people, they understand themselves to be fundamentally different from "unsaved" Jews. Thus, Messianic Jews seek to actuate two messages: "We are *Jews*!" "We are *Messianic* Jews!" The different emphases, on "Jew" and "Messianic," describe the tension that leads not just to an affirmation of American Jewish identity, but also to a transformation of that identity to fit the new image of a "saved" Jew.

However, not all Messianic believers *are* Jews. Nothing is as problematic as the large number of Messianic Gentiles in the movement. To claim Jewish identity when one is not Jewish oneself adds another layer of struggle: "We are *Jews*!" "We are *Messianic* Jews!" "We are Messianic *Gentiles/spiritual* Jews!"[2]

I only recently discovered my identity as a Messianic Gentile when I heard the term for the first time from a speaker at the 2018 MJAA Summer conference (Messianic Jewish Alliance of America). I had been in and out of the Messianic Judaism movement since 2004 and was renewing my faith with three days at the conference. The first day, in response to my remark

1. Harris-Shapiro, *Messianic Judaism*, 14–15.
2. Harris-Shapiro, *Messianic Judaism*, 15.

that the session on Messianic prophecy sounded like Christian teaching with its stress on the Incarnation, I was asked for the first time in my life if I was Jewish. Revealing that I was not seemed to confirm something to the professor I had approached, perhaps that the concern I had voiced was that of a Gentile and not of a converted Jew.

No and Yes

The flag I was raising in my mind those three days accentuated the distinction, so basic and yet so difficult for Messianic Judaism, between being a part of the church as one more denomination of Christianity or being apart from the church as a distinct body of believers who:

- do not confess the Apostles' Creed or the Nicene Creed;
- do not celebrate, in a traditional way, the sacraments of the church: baptism and Holy Communion;
- do not use aides for devotion such as crosses, icons, or rosaries;
- do not follow the calendar of the seasons of the church, including Lent and Easter or Advent and Christmas;
- do not follow the Revised Common Lectionary;
- do not participate in ecumenical ministries such as the World Council of Churches;
- do not embrace church history; and
- do not have Christian weddings or funerals.

Messianic Judaism decidedly professes the latter: to be separate from the church, not a Hebrew Christian denomination. At the same time, we arbitrarily embrace key tenants of Protestant Christianity. We have the New Testament, the eschatology, the doctrines of Providence and election, the doctrine of salvation by the atonement of Yeshua—all contributions of the church since the fourth century if not since the first century—and yet, we still do not see ourselves as "Christians."

Hebrew/Jewish Christians were there at the beginning and into the twenty-first century as self-identified believers in the Christ of the church and the creeds. The evangelistic ministry of Jews for Jesus continues to bring Jews into a saving relationship with Jesus Christ and into the baptism of the church. Jewish people convert in every generation. In the 1970s, Keith Green and Bob Dylan became Christians while Jewish. How are Messianic Jews distinguishing themselves from this conventional understanding?

They do so in a variety of ways. A Messianic rabbi from Kentucky at the MJAA conference said the defining idea is the kingdom of God and that Messianic Jews and Christians have different ways of being in the kingdom. But does it make sense to say that I have decided to join the kingdom of God and become a member? Can I remember the kingdom of God in my will? The concept is too elastic. On the other hand, some Messianic Jews are too narrow in their dispensationalism, displacing both Jews and Christians as the chosen vehicle for God's activity in the end times. The idea is that not only should all Jews join our Messianic movement but so should all Christians by redefining themselves by our Messianic Jewish lights. There is one true faith and we are it.[3]

A Voice in the Night

I have a different idea about the truth in Messianic Judaism that has come through reflection on my own experience with God. Without prior warning my God converted from Christianity to Messianic Judaism and took me with him. I have been trying to understand it ever since and in writing this book have discovered some answers. Thomas Merton once wrote, "On all sides I am confronted by questions that I cannot answer, because the time for answering them has not yet come."[4] Messianic Judaism has been this kind of a confrontation to me, and the time for answering has taken years.

Until my first visit to a Messianic synagogue—Beit HaTorah in Elkton, Maryland—I was an outsider who did not care enough to have an opinion. Then in three swift movements of the Holy Spirit, I was thrust to the inside, made a Messianic Gentile newborn to the faith of Messianic Judaism.

---

3. David H. Stern calls for the church to remake itself as a part of our movement: "Christians must learn—whether from Ruth or from Paul—that in Jesus they become part of a great big Jewish family, and it is within this family relationship that they find God, along with his covenants, promises and hope. This is what is meant by the olive tree metaphor of Romans 11:17–24, which says that Gentile 'wild branches' have been grafted into God's olive tree (the Jewish people) among the natural branches (Jews). What is spoken of here is not mystical but practical. Through faith in the Jewish Messiah a Gentile can have God-enhanced, God-blessed human relationships with Jews and with other Gentiles who have found Yeshua and accept him as the atonement for their sins, as well as with Jews who haven't yet accepted him. If Jews fail to welcome Christians as 'family,' it's not the fault of the Jews but the fault of Christians who do not understand who they really are in Messiah Yeshua! And it therefore becomes the Christians' responsibility to re-think their identity so that they can do whatever will be necessary to undo centuries of misunderstanding between Jews and Christians and ultimately to make real their closeness and identification with the Jewish people." Stern, *Restoring the Jewishness of the Gospel*, 76.

4. Merton, "Fire Watch, July 4, 1952," 215.

I practiced it privately for three years, only telling my family along with members of the Messianic congregation. When I first got up the nerve to tell my wife I was converting from Christianity to Messianic Judaism, she told me I wasn't, and then she began to cry. My teenage children handled it in stride. I did not confide to anyone in my Presbyterian congregations (PCUSA), two small churches in Delaware City and Port Penn, Delaware. I continued as their pastor as I always had, except I was busy with something else on Saturdays. Rather than try and bring them along on my spiritual journey I settled on the idea that the calling I had to Messianic Judaism was for me and not my congregations or my family.

It began with a sense of being addressed by an inner voice that I recognized from past experience as God or the Holy Spirit. Two words were conveyed: "Go there." I was looking at the ad for the Beit HaTorah synagogue on the church page of the *Cecil Whig*, the daily newspaper of Elkton, Maryland. Even though I lived in Delaware I had joined the board of directors of Meeting Ground, a ministry to homeless persons based in Cecil County, Maryland. So I was passing the time volunteering at our shelter when I picked up the paper. I left that night with a mission: Go there.

A Messianic Revelation

It was not hard to find, being on State Route 40 outside of Elkton. The building had once been a restaurant and was converted into worship space. I was greeted warmly, and I introduced myself to a couple of people as a pastor who was interested in learning about their ministry. I sat by myself in a row of folded chairs towards the back. I really was not wondering why I was there. I just accepted that this was something I was supposed to do. Once and done was probably my idea. The service went along and then the inner voice spoke once again. A question: "What's the last verse of the Tanakh?" I had either seen some Tanakhs on a bookshelf, or I now noticed them there. I knew the last verse of Malachi in the Old Testament was about Elijah, and I also knew the Tanakh was in a different order from the Old Testament, so it had a different last verse. Before I left, I was going to look up that verse.

That was much on my mind as the service ended, and I prepared to exit. I didn't know where else I could find a Tanakh except right where I was. But I was being polite to greet everyone nearby. A visitor to a small congregation—there were thirty or forty people—draws attention. Then the rabbi, Sariella Creeger, approached to give me her personal greeting. After she introduced herself, she said that the woman with her, Atira, was a prophet, and she wanted to speak to me because the Lord had given her a word for me. She had written it down because she wanted to get it right.

It was two sides of a small piece of paper that she gave to me after she read it aloud. I kept it for many years and must have left it behind in some book. It was for the pastor. The thrust was that I was to follow the ways of God and not the ways of man. And I was not to be theological. Ask and I would receive. I took the note and thanked Atira. The rabbi expressed appreciation for my openness to it. When I read the closing verses of 2 Chronicles on the last page of the Tanakh I knew for certain that the prophetic word from Atira and the direction of the inner voice were in sync. The Tanakh ends with a call by a Gentile to come up to Jerusalem.

The directive to not be theological recalled to me the name of my seminary: Princeton Theological Seminary. "Theological" was about my ordination to ministry in the Presbyterian Church (USA). "Theological" was about Western thinking: as in Augustine, Aquinas, Luther, Calvin, Kierkegaard, and Barth. The Torah was decidedly non-Western and non-theological. I was being called to leave behind one way of relating to God and take up another. In hindsight, I would say I was being told to change religions.

Meeting Jesus Again for the First Time

In her memoir, *The Light Within Me*, Ainsley Earhardt recalls making this prayer:

> God, I don't know how to do this but I want you in my life. I am willing to give up all of this, the smoking and the drinking and everything else. You must already be taking that away from me because I don't want to do it anymore. I want whatever else is out there. I want this void in my life filled forever . . . I want it filled with you.[5]

That is how the prayer is published, but when you listen to Ainsley Earhardt reading the audiobook she changes the wording to make it a prayer to Jesus: *"Jesus, I don't know how to do this but I want you in my life."* The title of the chapter, "Meeting Jesus at a Frat Party," indicates that the audio version may be the truer recollection and that perhaps an editor inserted "God" in place of "Jesus" for the HarperCollins publication to have an inclusive prayer. The difference is semantic, stylistic, and also theological. If Jewish readers were to identify with this prayer to Jesus they would be trespassing into false religion and blasphemy.

---

5. Earhardt, *The Light Within Me*, 36.

As a Presbyterian, I could pray either way. Prayer to Jesus was as good as prayer to God. In Christianity, the Trinity of Father, Son, and Holy Spirit is God, God, God. But when I was told to no longer be theological and to no longer follow the path I had been on, because now I was to change somehow, I was told to recognize a prayer to Jesus as polytheistic and non-Jewish.

Praying the psalms—"The LORD is my shepherd" or "I lift up mine eyes unto the hills, from whence cometh my help"(KJV)—was not to include thoughts of Jesus. I would let go of Christian prayer in the course of time. But to do so was the prophetic word I received that first day. That is what it meant to go up to Jerusalem.

Bart D. Ehrman, in a lecture asking, "Did Jesus Think He was God?" states these truths:

> In ancient Jewish tradition there was a term for the future king of Israel. The term was messiah. The messiah was not supposed to be God. The messiah was going to be a human. There were no Jews in the ancient world that taught the messiah was God. The messiah was a human being.[6]

This is how God was revealing Jesus (Yeshua) to me: as a man among men, always human, always the chosen one of us but always one of us. He did all that he did as a human being like other great men of the Bible. By his death he made intercession and cut a new covenant with atonement for sin. I adore him for that. Now he lives and is exalted in the heavens—but not as divine.

This is not Christianity. Neither is it Judaism. It is an expression of Messianic Judaism. I came to it out of my twenty-two-year experience as a Presbyterian minister who preached the miracles of the Old Testament just as easily as the miracles of the New Testament. I was also acquainted with the prerogative of adopting and adapting another religion's scriptures on a selective basis. This is done in the church by shifting the Sabbath to Sunday, reading from the book of Psalms for Christian funerals, and by elevating the scriptural basis for tithing above the other directives for keeping a Jewish lifestyle in the verses that surround it. In turn, Messianic Jews must adopt and adapt the Christian scriptures to suit their inspired vision the way Christians do with the Hebrew Bible. So I now realize there are a variety of Christologies in the New Testament and the highest of them does not suit Messianic Judaism.

---

6. Ehrman, "Did Jesus Think He Was God?"

The Training Kicks In

Along with familiarity with Christology and biblical interpretation, I came to my conversion equipped with a respect for Judaism as a biblical religion that operates on its own merits and own covenants. I adopted this point of view as a part of my ministerial training. In 1987, the Presbyterian Church (USA) published a document from our General Assembly that elevated Christian-Jewish relations to the level of a partnership of equals. Entitled *A Theological Understanding of the Relationship Between Christians and Jews*, it includes seven affirmations:

1. a reaffirmation that the God who addresses both Christians and Jews is the same—the living and true God;
2. a new understanding by the church that its own identity is intimately related to the continuing identity of the Jewish people;
3. a willingness to ponder with Jews the mystery of God's election of both Jews and Christians to be a light to the nations;
4. an acknowledgement by Christians that Jews are in covenant relationship with God and the consideration of the implications of this reality for evangelism and witness;
5. a determination by Christians to put an end to "the teaching of contempt" for the Jews;
6. a willingness to investigate the continuing significance of the promise of "land," and its associated obligations and to explore the implications for Christian theology;
7. a readiness to act on the hope which we share with the Jews in God's promise of the peaceable kingdom.[7]

The implication for evangelism was to reframe it as a dialogue:

> Hence, when speaking with Jews about matters of faith, we must always acknowledge that Jews are already in a covenantal relationship with God.[8]
>
> Dialogue is the appropriate form of faithful conversation between Christians and Jews. Dialogue is not a cover for proselytism. Rather, as trust is established, not only questions and concerns can be shared but faith and commitments as well.[9]

---

7. Office of the General Assembly, "A Theological Understanding," 4.
8. Office of the General Assembly, "A Theological Understanding," 10.
9. Office of the General Assembly, "A Theological Understanding," 12.

So my confrontation with Messianic Judaism was, in one sense, a leap from reliance on the new covenant as a Christian to reliance on both the new covenant and the other biblical covenants. Unlike Messianic Jews who seem to have a sense of leaving behind their reliance on the traditional Jewish covenants in order to embrace the new one in Yeshua, I felt the opposite. Not that this made me Jewish. But Messianic Judaism opened a door for me to participate in the covenants of God in a way that had not been possible in Christianity.

How God Finds Us

So I was no longer going to be a Christian. I left the ministry and the presbytery removed my name from their roll. I went to work for a different homeless ministry in Wilmington, Delaware and for several years managed a half-way house for men in recovery. Things changed at Beit HaTorah, and after being away a year in India, I did not reconnect. But I had this book that would not let go of me, and I worked on it over the years, going back to church services at the same time. Then I went to the MJAA conference for three days, and it relit the fire and the vision. I needed to put Yeshua back into his humanity and try being Messianic instead of just reflecting on its meaning. So I quit attending church again and sought out another Messianic Jewish congregation: Rosh Pina in Owings Mills, Maryland.

This conversion story is in just about the reverse direction of other Messianic Jewish testimonies. Most of the published works on Messianic Judaism arise from a Jewish mind and heart, a Jewish perspective and experience, as can be seen from online searches and at the book tables of Messianic Jewish conferences. The answers in them generally arise out of questions that confront Jews. Some of the answers suggest—like when my MJAA Jewish colleague answered my question with a question about my ethnicity—that non-Jewish opinions may not be equally valued. But I was embraced warmly in my years at the Beit HaTorah congregation and several times invited to teach from the Torah portion. This book has its origin in our Jewish rabbi's request that I write an introduction to Messianic Judaism for new believers and interested outsiders.

A conversion must be a matter of integrity. As Martin Luther famously asserted concerning his new faith: "Here I stand. I cannot do otherwise. God help me. Amen."[10] My story involves figuring out what just happened and what it is I have embraced: a movement in the church? Jewish Christianity? A new school of Judaism? The kingdom of God? Most improbably it is a

---

10. Bainton, *Here I Stand*, 400.

new religion, a new way of relating to the God of the Bible. Not because we needed it or thought of it or wanted it, but because God is acting this way.

God finds us as Messianic Jews and Messianic Gentiles. He is the God of the Bible revealing himself in a new way that is neither Christianity nor Judaism—revealing, choosing, anointing, healing, teaching, guiding, redeeming and saving. Ultimately it is not about us, it is about him. So Karl Barth wrote from his Christian perspective in words that resonate with the truth of Messianic Judaism:

> It is not the right human thoughts about God which form the content of the Bible, but the right divine thoughts about men. The Bible tells us not how we should talk with God but what he says to us; not how we find the way to him, but how he has sought and found the way to us; not the right relationship in which we must place ourselves to him, but the covenant which he has made with all who are Abraham's spiritual children and which he has sealed once and for all in Jesus Christ. It is this which is within the Bible. The word of God is within the Bible.[11]

Progressive Revelation

We normally think of God calling us forward, and we want to imagine that whatever God has for us in the future is something better than we have been living with. But how could I tell my Christian congregations, my Christmas-and-Easter friends and family, my Presbyterian colleagues in the gospel ministry, that I was leaving them behind with their Christianity for something better? I was excited that way. But it was awkward, and I left the people who cared enough to wonder about me to make up their own minds. Off I went.

In the Conclusion to this book you will read about a word of prophecy given by an Oklahoma City minister to a Messianic Jewish rabbi from Toronto at a pastors' conference where the gifts of the Holy Spirit were manifested. This is one sentence that the rabbi, Jeff Forman, repeated to the 2018 MJAA Conference:

> The Nicodemus anointing that's been there, that you have come by night to get the information you needed—God's about to remove you from the side street to the Main Street

---

11. Barth, "The Strange New World," 43.

because the kingdom of David and the throne of David are being restored in this generation.[12]

Now it is presumptuous to argue with a word from God given by the Holy Spirit, but the idea of "the Nicodemus anointing that's been there" suggests to me that Jews, in and of themselves in their religion, are incomplete followers of God and need to embrace the Christian gospel to be completed. It is captured in the designation "Old Testament" for their scriptures. Jews never have used that title. It was imposed upon their sacred writings by another religion, Christianity.

At the same time Christians rewarded themselves with the designation of "New Testament" for their holy texts. Worse, they usurped, wrested, absorbed, and unapologetically expropriated the story and identity and covenants and psalms of the Hebrew people. Here is a prominent Calvin scholar, Wilhelm Niesel, explaining how this can be done by a top-notch Christian theologian:

> A theologian such as Calvin does not understand the relationship of the two Testaments in such wise that he reads the Old into the New and vice versa. Certainly he used the one to elucidate the other. But that is not the important thing. The decisive point is the recognition that the Old Testament promises what the New Testament offers to us in Christ. The salvation of the saints of the Old Testament is founded, just as much as our own, in Jesus Christ. Therefore in both cases what is in question is the one "body of Christ—the church"; the new covenant is no other than the old covenant instituted by God and broken by the people of Israel. Christ is the foundation of the divine covenant to which both the Old Testament and the New bear witness.[13]

Did you catch the bait-and-switch that made Israel's historic covenants disappear? It is in the last sentence with the introduction of something new, "the divine covenant," that is more than any one historical covenant, all of which are now only so much filler or details to the divine covenant God has made with . . . whom? The Christians? The world? Are the disobedient Jews simply left behind with their broken remnants? Or, like "the saints of the Old Testament," have they become Christians too?

Messianic Judaism is not about redeeming the "old" religion of Judaism. Nor is it a fresh display of Christianity. It is something new, newer than Judaism and newer than Christianity. Newer than the new. Because God

---

12. Forman, et al., "Erev Shabbat."
13 Niesel, *Theology of Calvin*, 105.

does not slumber: "Behold, he that keepeth Israel shall neither slumber nor sleep" (Ps 121:4 KJV). Messianic believers are as incomplete and stumbling along as is everyone else. But God is blessing us to be a blessing. We will bless the world, including the Jews and Christians to whom we are indebted for scriptures and traditions that we carry with us on our journey forward.

2

Airing Our Linen

The *Wikipedia* article on Messianic Judaism is comprehensive and cluttered with details, including three mentions of the Messianic Jews who do not believe in the divinity of Jesus.[1] This is my tribe. I am joining the minority because joining the majority would have made no essential difference from my Christian commitments. In sending me to Beit HaTorah ("House of Torah") God was telling me to make a change. From this point of view, I now look over the landscape of Messianic Judaism and offer a direction for growth and prosperity.

Making News

According to Joel Willitts it is an exciting time to be a Messianic Jew because the faith is still being revealed, and the story is still unfolding. Willitts is one editor of a fulsome compendium of essays entitled *Introduction to Messianic Judaism*. He has the last word in the final chapter and offers seven observations:

1. Messianic Judaism is historically both ancient and modern.
2. Messianic Judaism is a multilingual, worldwide movement of Messianic Jews and Messianic Gentiles who have come alongside them.

---

1. Wikipedia, s.v., "Messianic Judaism."

3. Messianic Judaism is a diverse movement theologically, culturally, halachically, and ecclesially.
4. Messianic Judaism is a growing movement that remains very much in process.
5. Messianic Judaism is in the midst of an intense period of identity formation.
6. Messianic Judaism is developing young leaders who are theologically and biblically trained at the highest levels, ensuring a strong future.
7. Messianic Judaism is experiencing positive development in its relationship with the wider Jewish and Christian worlds.[2]

The excitement and controversy that is news is sandwiched in the middle observations, numbers three, four, and five. This is where the energy and anticipation are:

- Can the creative tension in the diverse movement be sustained?
- Or will the movement coalesce around one expression, either in the direction of membership in the Body of Christ or in the opposite direction of another branch of Judaism?
- How many sides or factions are at work in this movement, what dynamics are driving it, and what messages are shaping its agenda?
- Can a consensus be built for a third religion with its own grounds of salvation that are not identical with either of the two traditional biblical religions?

Roots

Richard Harvey credits David Rausch for "a pioneering study of the modern movement" in 1982: *Messianic Judaism: Its History, Theology and Polity*.[3] Harvey observes that one of Rausch's descriptions, on the fundamentalist character of Messianic Judaism, has held true over the decades:

> Rausch had previously studied American Fundamentalism and was 'immediately drawn to the correlations between both theologies'. After 'many hundreds' of interviews with Messianic Jews he concludes that 'their theology is that of the Fundamentalist/ Evangelical movement in which Hebrew Christian theology is

2. Willitts, "Conclusion," 316–17.
3. Harvey, *Mapping Messianic Jewish Theology*, 29.

rooted'. The characterization of Messianic Judaism as a Jewish-flavoured variant of North American Fundamentalism is the main explanatory model. Rausch accurately describes Messianic Judaism in the late 1970s and early 1980s, many of whose features have been maintained up to the present.[4]

Harvey then qualifies this conclusion by noting the diversity of opinion—some critical—with which Rausch's work was first received. "Fundamentalism" can be a sloppy label which substitutes for genuine analysis but "evangelical" is far within the mark for the Messianic Jewish Alliance of America (MJAA). The Union of Messianic Jewish Congregations (UMJC), whose statement of faith is cited in the Introduction, also identifies with the church. So whether the pole holding down the Christian end of the tension within Messianic Judaism is fundamentalist or evangelical hardly matters in light of the explicit denials at the other end of the polarity of core tenants of Christianity.

The Non-Christian Yeshua

Consider these statements by leaders of Messianic Jewish congregations in the light of traditional Christian doctrine. Two were published in *Israel Today* magazine in 2001, and the third is from the personal correspondence which appears in chapter 8:

> There are 53 places in the New Testament where we read that there is only one God. Those who teach a faith involving several gods are praying to foreign gods. Anyone who wants to make Yeshua into God has lost his way on his journey of faith. Whether Yeshua is God or not depends on this question: how do we explain God?—Joseph Shulam in Jerusalem.[5]

> Yeshua Ha'Mashiach is not God, he is the Son of God and the Redeemer. There are countless verses that state very clearly that Yeshua is not God. Even if Yeshua says that He and the Father are One, Yeshua also says in the same chapter that not only is He one with His Father but we are also one with the Father. Does that mean that we are God as well? The Trinity is completely pagan. On the cross Yeshua cried out, *"Eli Eli (My God), why have You forsaken Me?* Does God turn to God? Can one nail a God to a cross? Millions of people were murdered because they were

---

4. Harvey, *Mapping Messianic Jewish Theology*, 29.
5. Schneider, "Messianic Jews Debate," 21.

accused of killing God, and what were their last words? "Hear O Israel, the Lord our God, the Lord is one." Can this be Yeshua's theology?—David Tel Tzur in Ma'ale Adumim.[6]

In Revelation 3:12 Y'shua calls G-d *his* G-d no less than 4 times. If G-d can have a G-d would that not make two gods? And would not the god that Y'shua served be a greater god then himself? This is pure polytheism. We believe in One indivisible G-d who is the Eternal and who even Y'shu called the only true G-d in John 17:3 where he says *"This is eternal life that they might know you the only true G-d and Y'shua HaMashiach whom you sent."* It is very clear that Y'shua knew who G-d was and he did not claim to be that G-d.—Adam Yisroel.[7]

What fellowship can these men have with conservative evangelical Messianic Jews, such as those trained at Moody Bible Institute or Dallas Theological Seminary or The King's University—Christian institutions which welcome Messianic Jews who believe, as they do, in the divinity of Yeshua and the triune nature of God? If they are heretical and unsaved by the lights of Christianity can the judgment of like-minded Messianic Jews be less severe?

Richard Harvey asked one of the founders of the Messianic movement, David Stern, about a dialogue between opposing sides after *Israel Today* published those two heterodox statements alongside more orthodox ones in an article, "Messianic Jews Debate the Deity of Jesus." Stern responded in a 2003 email:

> So far as I know, there is no fuller report of these discussions. The sense of the meeting of the leaders that brought the problem to wide attention was that it would be better not to air our laundry (clean or dirty, as the case may have been).[8]

I missed that discussion and debate of 2002/2003, but as of 2020, the tension in Messianic Judaism is still with us. The burden of this book is to kindle some light where there is mystery, to elevate what is essential for success, and to offer solutions to some of the knotty problems that continue to accompany the Messianic Jewish movement.

---

6. Schneider, "Messianic Jews Debate," 21.
7. Personal correspondence with the author.
8. Harvey, *Mapping Messianic Jewish Theology*, 98.

Reading the Bible Together

Joel Willitts writes,

> My interest in Messianic Judaism, as for most things in life, is the result of relationship. In this case, there are two relationships in particular: my relationship to the text and context of the New Testament and my relationship with David Rudolph, my co-editor.[9]

Any theology of Messianic Judaism would be, and ought to be, judged according to the biblical text. Any rule for congregational life should be evaluated according to the text. And any soteriology of Messianic Judaism, likewise, will stand or fall according to the text. What is decisive in reading the biblical text together is a mutual respect, regardless of the assumptions about the text that people may bring. A widespread assumption is the infallibility of scripture. According to Daniel Juster, "The Messianic Jewish community shares with Orthodox Judaism and conservative evangelical Christianity, the view that the Bible is infallible. This is, for example, enshrined in the statements of belief of both the UMJC and the IAMCS, the two largest associations of Messianic Jewish Congregations in the world."[10]

Now consider this passage from a former professor at Dallas Theological Seminary, Roy B. Zuck, who holds this same belief. In his book *Basic Bible Interpretation* he draws a boundary line:

> *Qualifications for Interpreting the Bible*
> No one can fully comprehend the meaning of the Bible unless he is regenerate. The unsaved person is spiritually blind (2 Cor. 4:4) and dead (Eph. 2:2). Paul wrote, "The man without the Spirit does not accept the things that come from the Spirit of God, for they are foolishness to him, and he cannot understand them, because they are spiritually discerned" (1 Cor. 2:14). Does this mean an unsaved person cannot understand the words of Scripture? No. Instead it means he has no spiritual capacity for welcoming and appropriating spiritual truths. As Martin Luther once said, the unregenerate can understand the grammar of John 3:16, but they do not act on those facts. It is in this sense that they are unable to know the things of the Spirit of God.
> First Corinthians 2:14 also states that the unsaved do not "understand spiritual things." The Greek word *ginosko* ("to understand") does not mean comprehend intellectually; it means

---

9. Willitts, "Conclusion," 315.
10. Juster, "Biblical Authority," 19.

know by experience. The unsaved obviously do not experience God's Word because they do not welcome it. Only the regenerate have the capacity to welcome and experience the Scriptures, by means of the Holy Spirit.[11]

This is representative of a tradition. Conservative evangelicals, whether Christian or Messianic, consider people to be unregenerate, unsaved, and outside the plan and purpose of God who do not embrace the traditional, orthodox teachings of the New Testament. That leaves both Jews and the Messianic Jewish minority, who reject the Incarnation and Trinity, out of fellowship, away from the table, and separated from the saved and the spiritually-minded.

Too Easily Scandalized

But the Jews and the Messianic Jews who reject the Incarnation and Trinity will not go away. For two thousand years, conservative evangelical Christians have been waiting for the Jews to go away, either by conversion or assimilation, and they have not. To the embarrassment, perhaps, of the MJAA and UMJC, Messianic Jews insisting on both their Judaism and their human Yeshua are not disappearing either.

The current majority in the Messianic movement is intolerant of a lot:

- People calling themselves Messianic Jews who show up denying the divinity of Yeshua are one sort of embarrassment to other Messianic Jews who declare it.[12]

- Another sort of embarrassment to these same evangelical Messianic Jews is, of course, the unsaved Jews themselves who explicitly reject Yeshua and everything that goes with him.

- On the other side are other believers in the Incarnation and Trinity who formulated those doctrines and preserved the New Testament— the Roman Catholic Church with its pope and church teaching and

---

11. Zuck, *Basic Bible Interpretation*, 22–23.

12. Harvey notes, "Previous studies have emphasized the uniformity of the orthodox (Christian) Christologies within Messianic Judaism. The presence of heterodox views has caused some embarrassment within the movement." Harvey, *Mapping Messianic Jewish Theology*, 103–4. Sam Nadler instructs, "Messianic believers who believe we are under Mosaic *torah* seek to be faithful—but they are guarding the wrong bridge. The truth of the Good News of Yeshua is the bridge that leads home, and it is the bridge we are called to guard." Nadler, *Messianic Foundations*, 201.

priests and monasteries and cathedrals: all an embarrassment to Jewish evangelical sensibilities.[13]

- The embarrassment of a Gentilized church would extend further in the direction of the Orthodox churches with their icons and incense and saint's days;
- As well as in the direction of mainstream Protestant churches with their liberation theology, feminism, inclusiveness of gays and lesbians, and critical study of the Bible.

Who in the world is not an embarrassment to the conscience of fundamentalist/evangelical/charismatic/conservative Messianic Jews? How small is their ark of salvation by which the world will be saved in the last days?

To get to the text and the context of the New Testament together we must have mutual respect and not decide ahead of time that we will only listen to opinions with which we already agree. The kindness we hope for is the goodwill to believe that we all want the will of God to be manifest and accomplished.

The Creative Self-Disclosure of God

Anglican churchman Austin Farrer, preaching on one of Christ's parables, said this:

> Theologians have no claim whatever to be pleased with themselves, for, unlike the scientist, the theologian makes no discoveries: he merely interprets and relays the self-disclosure of God. A scientist may be a creative genius: not so a theologian. So God paints the picture, and God explains the effect at which he aims; he opens our eyes to it.[14]

The Messianic movement is not awaiting better leadership, better followers, better teaching, better music, or better books to fulfill its potential. It is awaiting an act of God. We want the picture that God paints, not our best idea of what that should be. The task is discernment. Faith, courage, and intelligence will be needed to accomplish it.

---

13. Stern writes, "When the Church proclaims a Gospel without its Jewishness restored, she is at best failing to proclaim 'the whole counsel of God' (Acts 20:27). At worst she may be communicating what is called 'another Gospel' (Galatians 1:6–9)" Stern, *Restoring the Jewishness of the Gospel*, ix.

14. Farrer, "The Painter's Colours," 2.

Joel Willitts offers an example of making sense in a new Messianic way. He writes:

> Second, *Introduction to Messianic Judaism* introduces a post-supersessionist reading of the New Testament. Most Christians naturally read the Bible in a supersessionist way. Such an approach is largely unintentional for most. It is the by-product of uncritical assumptions concerning what the Scriptures teach about the Jewish people. *Introduction to Messianic Judaism* offers a new paradigm for reading the Bible, one that is more consistent with its message of the fulfillment of Israel's story in the story of Jesus, Israel's Messiah.[15]

It is a commonplace among Christians that the New Testament and its covenant and people superseded the Old Testament and its covenants and people. Willitts is appealing for a hermeneutic that honors the legitimacy of the Jewish religion and nation.

Many of us, from the late sixties to the present, are attracted to the idea of God doing a new thing through Messianic Judaism. For some it is in belonging. For some it is in personal devotion. For some it is in worship. For some it is in reading the Bible. God is painting his picture of us in all these ways but it is in Bible reading—in building a relationship to the text and context of the Bible—that Messianic Judaism will ultimately stand or fall.

New paradigms, such as a post-supersessionist reading of the New Testament, are our best hope if the hope is something other than being a part of the church. If the burden is to save the church from its error, then joining the church with integrity as Jewish converts may relieve that burden. But if instead Messianic Jews and Gentiles discern God doing something new apart from his work in the church we will look for new paradigms to read the Bible in the way he has opened our eyes to see.

A Case Study

To explore the idea of a Messianic hermeneutic let us start with the Christian hermeneutic and Psalm 51:

> Have mercy on me, O God,
> according to your unfailing love;
> according to your great compassion
> blot out my transgressions.
> ² Wash away all my iniquity

---

15. Willitts, "Conclusion," 318.

and cleanse me from my sin.
³ For I know my transgressions,
and my sin is always before me.
⁴ Against you, you only, have I sinned
and done what is evil in your sight;
so you are right in your verdict
and justified when you judge.
⁵ Surely I was sinful at birth,
sinful from the time my mother conceived me.
⁶ Yet you desired faithfulness even in the womb;
you taught me wisdom in that secret place.
⁷ Cleanse me with hyssop, and I will be clean;
wash me, and I will be whiter than snow.
⁸ Let me hear joy and gladness;
let the bones you have crushed rejoice.
⁹ Hide your face from my sins
and blot out all my iniquity.
¹⁰ Create in me a pure heart, O God,
and renew a steadfast spirit within me.
¹¹ Do not cast me from your presence
or take your Holy Spirit from me.
¹² Restore to me the joy of your salvation
and grant me a willing spirit, to sustain me.
¹³ Then I will teach transgressors your ways,
so that sinners will turn back to you.
¹⁴ Deliver me from the guilt of bloodshed, O God,
you who are God my Savior,
and my tongue will sing of your righteousness.
¹⁵ Open my lips, Lord,
and my mouth will declare your praise.
¹⁶ You do not delight in sacrifice, or I would bring it;
you do not take pleasure in burnt offerings.
¹⁷ My sacrifice, O God, is a broken spirit;
a broken and contrite heart
you, God, will not despise.
¹⁸ May it please you to prosper Zion,
to build up the walls of Jerusalem.
¹⁹ Then you will delight in the sacrifices of the righteous,
in burnt offerings offered whole;
then bulls will be offered on your altar.

This is not a Messianic psalm. It addresses God apart from his revelation in Jesus Christ, in the New Testament and in the cross of Christ. Of course, it was written centuries before those acts of God. Yet here in the Hebrew Bible a sinner is in the process of being washed clean of all his iniquity, if his plea is heard. Because this prayer was preserved and regarded as scripture we certainly think it was answered and that the psalmist was saved and cleansed and God did grant him a pure heart and even the gift of the Holy Spirit.

How is this witness authentic for a Christian who is taught to find being saved and forgiven of sin in the atoning sacrifice of Jesus, as described in the New Testament? Psalm 51:11 is not anticipating Acts 2 and the day of Pentecost for an experience of the Holy Spirit. But the church does. How can Christians make sense of appropriating the Jews' Psalm 51 for themselves?

It is a matter of a Christian hermeneutic founded on a set of assumptions about the church, the Jews, and the Hebrew scriptures. A Christian starts reading the Old Testament through the lens and paradigm of the New Testament. The conceptual order for a Christian Bible is to begin the New Testament on page one and then follow Revelation with the book of Genesis into the second half of their Bible. They interpret the sin and salvation in Psalm 51 according to Christian categories. As Christians, they know what sin is. They know what salvation is. They define their terms and project those definitions onto the Hebrew Bible.

How Eyes Open to a New Picture

A Messianic hermeneutic does the same. We define our terms according to the revelation in the Torah and the Hebrew Bible and then read the New Testament with that lens. We read about God and atonement and covenant and Sabbath and commandments and prayer and forgiveness and righteousness and the last days and love and faith and worship and obedience and holiness—and we project those definitions onto the Christian scripture of the New Testament.

So Messianic rabbis Shulam and Tzur and Yisroel, quoted above, define God as one. That is a key to their understanding every occurrence of the terms God, son of God, son of the Blessed One, and throne of God in the pages of the gospels, the Acts of the Apostles, the epistles, and the Apocalypse. Monotheism is their paradigm. By that and other Jewish assumptions they appropriate the New Testament to fit with the Hebrew Bible in a Messianic way. In Willitt's phrase, they adopt a paradigm that is "more consistent with its message" for Messianic Jews.

For the first time Jews are reading the New Testament as scripture. It is a new experience, a new deal. It is not the experience of the church. We should not expect the church to agree with Messianic Judaism. The church does not share the same assumptions. If both faiths were the same, they would have common practice, which would include both the Apostles' Creed and the Amidah, as well as both Christmas and Passover. The hope of Messianic Judaism is that it is God's new thing, giving both the church and traditional Judaism some competition from the outside (or alongside).

Not Under Church Discipline

In fact, the assumption of a human Jesus is an old one, with a lineage that extends back to the beginnings of the church, in Ebionitism, Adoptionism and Arianism. This would make us heretics in the church. But we are not heretics simply because we are not in the church, under the church, or beholding to the church. We are non-Christians taking up the Christian sacred scriptures for our own use and understanding. The church can hardly complain about it since the church invented the idea of selective adoption and applied it to the Hebrew sacred writings.

We can follow the same pattern of appropriation that eliminates every individual difficulty by subordinating the entire secondary testament under the authority of the primary testament. In their case it was the Greek over the Hebrew. In our case it is the Hebrew over the Greek. In their case, by assuming Christianity is the completion of the plan and purpose of God begun with the Jews, contradictions to Christian ideas in the Jewish texts are easily dismissed as irrelevant in light of the new, better understanding. Such is the power of assumptions. In our case, Messianic Judaism has new understandings and interpretations that are better in our eyes.

It is important to preserve the canon and not reopen it for ourselves. We must arrogate to our religion all of the New Testament even as we read it selectively. Since the days of the Enlightenment and the Jefferson Bible, there have been those who would edit and splice out difficulties. That would be an error for Messianic Jews, as I argue in chapter 8. The whole Bible is our inheritance, even those parts that our understanding rejects as only Christian.

Discussion A:
When the Old Testament Isn't Old

Being non-Christian

"Messianic" and "Christian" are synonymous: one could also say "Christic" or "Messian" for the same reason. "The anointed" is the literal meaning. Translated to English from the Greek it comes out "Christ," and translated from the Hebrew it comes out "Messiah." So "Messianic Jew" does have the same sense as "Christian Jew." But we do not say "Jewish Messianic" or "Jewish Christian." Why? Because the primary meaning is in the noun, not the modifier, and the word "Christian" belongs to the church. Messianic Jews and Messianic Gentiles are not Christians. Instead, like Judaism, we relate to the church as another faith.

Now some Messianic Jews claim to be the true church in the sense that two thousand years of Christianity is a big misunderstanding from what God and Yeshua intended and that Messianic Jews now fulfill that intention. A common term in Messianic Jewish circles, adopted from the New Testament, is "the Body of Messiah," referring to what is translated from Greek as "the Body of Christ." Most Messianic Jews who claim to belong to the Body of Messiah also include Christians in it. They are trying to have it both ways: being the people of God as Jews and being the people of God as the church. Messianic Jews are not one or the other in the way most Jews and Christians commonly identify themselves.

A Covenant by Moshe

Read Deuteronomy 6.

Notice first the quotation marks embracing the whole chapter. Who is "me" in verse 1 but Moshe? The five books of the Torah are often titled "The Books of Moses." He is introduced in the second book as an exiled prince of Egypt being addressed by the God of Israel. Michael Fishbane observes:

> The mountain remains a mountain, and the bush a bush. But now all is changed: God has spoken to Moses. The words do not arise from within Moses. To the contrary; he is confronted and commanded by them ... Now, when God appears to him to fulfill the promise to the patriarchs (Exodus 3:6–8), Moses knows that he can never again return to his prior everyday activities. God's revelatory presence has driven a wedge into his lifetime and that of his brethren.[1]

The speech in Deuteronomy 6 is about extending this revelation given to Moshe to future generations. God's words came from without; they were discontinuous to everything going on in the world as well as everything going on in Moshe's life. This breakthrough, including the exodus from Egypt and the "commands, decrees and laws," must be carefully honored. Fishbane explains:

> The fathers are bidden by Moses to reveal their understanding of time and history to their sons. These latter must respond and answer for the sake of religious continuity. When God first spoke to Abram, and he responded, a new religious destiny entered history. His sons all accepted the commitment of their ancestor to a God who had first sent him into a new land with promises. Moses, himself a father of his people, continues this commitment during the dark days of the Egyptian bondage, and is enjoined to help bring the promises of the "god of the fathers" to fruition (Exodus 3:6–9; 6:2–8). Moses' commission is thus also an axial point along the way, as is the covenantal dedication of the entire people at Sinai. From the latter event on, continuity would depend not simply on divine grace and familial obligation but on an ongoing communal commitment to the covenant. As Moses teaches the covenant to the people, so each father is to teach its obligations to his own sons. In Deuteronomy 6:20–25, Moses forewarns future generations that

---

1. Fishbane, *Text and Texture*, 66.

everything would depend on the continuity of spiritual history. The response of the sons is not preserved.[2]

Discontinuity in the Church

Messianic Judaism claims its heritage in God's revelation to Moses (the Torah) as well as in God's revelation to Yeshua the Messiah. The church and Christianity do so as well. The Torah (sometimes translated in English as "the law" from the Greek word *nomos*) was adopted as sacred scripture and designated as the Old Testament in the church's Bible. But it is easy to see that the church has not maintained the continuity that Moshe asked for in Deuteronomy 6. The church adopted the books of Judaism and reinterpreted what it would mean to honor their truth. Literal obedience was rejected as an option of Christian observance. Another form of continuity was invented for Christian readers.

Now God is calling Messianic Jews to a literal obedience to the revelation of Moses along with honoring the revelation of Yeshua and the New Testament. The designations of the "Old Testament" and "the New Testament" are explicitly rejected even as their content is embraced. This is something new. This is a new religion.

Questions

1. Deuteronomy 6:4 begins, "Hear, O Israel . . ." What is your understanding of the Christian interpretation of this verse as applying to the church as well as to Jews?
2. Deuteronomy 6:25 concludes, "And if we are careful to obey all this law before the Lord our God, as he has commanded us, that will be our righteousness." What is your understanding of the Christian interpretation of this verse that rejects its application to the church?
3. How do you reconcile your answers to questions 1 and 2? If you cannot do it you may belong to the Messianic movement.

---

2. Fishbane, *Text and Texture*, 83.

3

The Messianic Heavenly Vision

Haftarah Lesson: Ezekiel 45:16—46:18
Beit HaTorah
March 24, 2012

Introduction

Usually when I am asked to teach at Beit HaTorah, I lead a meditation on the Torah portion, but this day I chose the Haftarah reading from the prophets because of Ezekiel's fantastic vision of another temple in Jerusalem with a prince of Israel performing the sacrifices. This is a Messianic heavenly vision comparable to Paul's heavenly vision at the foundation of Christianity. I lay the groundwork for this claim by arguing with Paul's curses on believers in Jesus who want to stay Torah observant. Messianic Jews are free to be Jews. Only in America could this possibility be realized in a new religion.

In God's Timing

I have a friend, Julia, who is 103 and lives in a nursing home in Middletown, Delaware. We visit once in a while and usually remember together our mutual friends from the Presbyterian church I once pastored. She was telling me about one of them, saying, "You've got to watch out when you see him coming. He won't stop talking." This is from a woman living in a wheelchair in a nursing home. She's talking about this friendly fellow named Jeff. "He will talk your ear off. We call him Jeff the Talker." Thinking that was funny, I replied, "Oh, and what do you call me?" Julia snapped right back, "You're Jeff the Jew."

The truth is my conversion to Messianic Judaism was both sudden and gradual. I knew after my first visit here that I was called to be here. But it was another three years before I resigned from my two churches and began belonging here exclusively. For those three years I did not tell anyone but my family that I was converting. I would come here for worship on Saturday and get up Sunday morning to preach and lead worship at my churches. I did not actually do that three consecutive years. I took time off from Beit HaTorah between the start in 2004 and the full embrace in 2007. I believed all the while I was in God's timing and in God's will, which is how I could keep the news of it from my congregations. My gospel ministry remained effective, I believe, partly because the congregations were not distracted by my faith journey into another religion.

The Rise of Messianic Judaism

Messianic Judaism is another religion from Christianity. That is not often emphasized or trumpeted. Maybe nobody is concerned about having a new kid on the block. Messianic Judaism is also, I believe, another religion from Judaism. We do not have to emphasize that to Jews. When they take notice they emphasize it to us. Except that the Jewish critics usually say we are a form of Christianity. We say we are a form of Judaism.

But what does it mean to embrace the New Testament—the *Brit Chadashah*—and not be a Christian? It used to mean that you were a heretic. In the Middle Ages heretics, such as the Cathari, were tortured by the church and sometimes burned at the stake for refusing to renounce their heresy. It would have cost something to be a Messianic Jew five hundred years ago. It cost to be a Jew. Those were the eras in Europe before pluralism and diversity were valued and appreciated. In America today you can be a Jehovah's Witness with your own English version of the New Testament, you can be a Mormon with your own idea of three gods in heaven as revealed in the scriptures of the Book of Mormon, or you can be a Messianic Jew fully embracing the Torah while claiming to follow the New Testament as well and no one will call you a heretic. In the case of Mormonism and Mitt Romney's presidential campaign, the popular media does not bother over the distinctions that make Mormonism a different religion from Christianity. It is not interested. Governor Romney says he believes in Jesus Christ and wants to leave it at that. So far America is going along. No doctrinal disputes about the Trinity here. No heresy here. No state church to enforce orthodoxy here. So Messianic Judaism rides in the wake of the waves in America's religious culture that Jehovah's Witnesses and Mormons have made in front of us.

That is generally how members of my congregations and members of my family have reacted to learning about my embrace of Messianic Judaism: as though I joined an off-beat religious option in American culture that they are not in a position to judge. I have enjoyed benign tolerance. If I am happy, they are happy for me. I know that some of you have paid more of a price to be here. I want to talk about why we do pay the price, why we are here, what God is calling you to in this place, in this religion.

Paul Detests His Jewish Opponents

Let us turn in our Bibles to Titus 1:10–16. Now someday, if you hear a Christian preacher describing you and your Messianic Jewish family as "detestable, disobedient and unfit for doing anything good" (Titus 1:16), you will know from where his inspiration came. What we are saying about Yeshua being the Living Torah and the words of the Torah being eternal truth is not that original. Our faith goes back to biblical times, to the days when the Bible was still being written. True, no one said it for almost two thousand years. But we are not original. We are an echo of believers in Yeshua who remained Torah observant in the first century. In Titus we see both how influential they once were—that their existence could raise such a serious and fervent response and they could be perceived as such a threat—and also how hopeless they were because there was only one Christ game in town. The fight was for all or nothing. No one imagined then that there could be two ways to follow Jesus, Yeshua: one in the church and one in Judaism. It would take America for such a thing to be possible and America was not going to be discovered for fifteen hundred years, with another three hundred years after that for religious tolerance to become the law of the land and the way of society.

So when the New Testament was being written and Sha'ul was laying the tracks for the church to follow, the truth was one thing, and you were right about it or you were wrong about it. Therefore Paul writes curses in his Letter to the Galatians on the people he perceived as his opponents. He is cursing us, really, in the way he understands Torah observance. For him, it is either/or. Galatians 2:21: "I do not nullify the grace of God; for if justification were through the law, then Christ died for nothing" (NRSV).

Well, I do not nullify the grace of God either. Maybe it depends upon what you mean by "justification," but I am called to join Messianic Jews who want to be Torah observant, even if I am not very good at it. No one here is saying that Christ died for no purpose. I do not contrast Christ dying with the law, with the Torah. Nor does the God I serve.

Both/And Instead of Either/Or

For one thing, there are Jews in heaven even if Christ did not die for them because all the promises of God to the Jews are true. Jesus never said, "My God, my God why have you forsaken the Jews?" Jesus never said, "Father, don't forgive the Jews for they know not what they do." Jesus never said, "Truly, I say to you, today and for the rest of eternity you Jews will never be with me in Paradise."

How did it happen that Paul conceived the rules of the Christ game to be all or nothing? Maybe because he was stoned in Lystra. Maybe because five times he received at the hands of the Jews the forty lashes less one. Countless beatings, he said. Often near death: "In danger from rivers, in danger from bandits, in danger from my fellow Jews" (2 Cor 11:26). He was Jewish himself so he could say: To hell with them. I wish they would go all the way and castrate themselves (Gal 5:12). You know, Sha'ul believed that Jesus was coming back soon from heaven. I wonder if he knew differently, if he knew the game would go on for centuries instead of years, whether he would have considered Judaism to be a legitimate religion that could exist along side the gospel and Christianity?

His version of all-or-nothing was universal. His version of either/or was a tower of Babel vision: everyone in the world worshipping one way. That way was not Judaism. Judaism was to give way to Christianity in his thinking.

Now in Romans 9—11, you find a softer side. Because when he bothers to think it through—when anybody bothers to think it through—you ultimately cannot say that the aim of Hitler, to do away with the Jews, was also the aim of Jesus, as the inspiration of Christianity. It is not the Jews who should castrate themselves, it is the Nazis. Don't curse the Jews, curse the enemies of the Jews. Bless the Jews.

That is what Jesus was about, blessing people. And he said his ministry was to the house of Israel. There is just no getting around the fact that Jesus himself was a Torah-observant Jew. Was he also detestable, disobedient and unfit for doing anything good (Titus 1:16)?

The witness of Messianic Judaism to the church—the reason God is raising us up as a family of God in our own right—is that you are not cursed if you choose to follow the law along with also embracing the atoning death of Jesus Christ, Yeshua HaMashiach. Come on in, the water is fine.

A Progressive Revelation

I believe that before God sent a messiah into the world to reveal God in a life he sent words into the world in the Hebrew language to reveal God in a scroll. In a book. In the Torah. And there is no contradiction in these two revelations. One is words of God, and the other is the man of God, the person of Yeshua. I do not have to give up one in order to embrace the other because for me they cannot be separated. I tell you they are the same truth, the same witness, the same power, and the same glory: both in time, both in history, both for eternity. Both have spiritual reality. Our vision is that they are the same spiritual reality.

Christianity has its heavenly vision. It is a light from heaven, brighter than the sun (Acts 9:1–9; 22:4–16; 26:9–18). It is Jesus, the risen messiah, breaking into history in the life of Paul. Our witness to Judaism is that we need not fear, we need not deny, we need not scorn this event, this heavenly vision of Yeshua. There is a progressive revelation of God in the world. For Messianic Jews, it makes sense to see God in the man Yeshua as we see God in the Torah. We do not separate Yeshua from the Torah. We do not separate the Torah from Yeshua.

It is not a matter of us having more than other Jews, just as it is not a matter of Christians having more than Jews. Of course God wills the advancement of Judaism for perpetuity, as long as the earth shall last. So God always wants there to be Jews who have nothing to do with Yeshua and Messianic Judaism. We are no more a universal salvation than Christianity or Judaism.

A Perfect Place With Real People

But God is doing a new thing in Messianic Judaism. We want to show the world, particularly the church I think, that there is a heavenly vision in the Hebrew Bible that can be embraced alongside Sha'ul's heavenly vision. I am thinking of the last nine chapters of the book of Ezekiel, which the prophet describes as a vision. Let us turn to Ezekiel 40: 1–4.

He tells us a lot of what he sees. He gives 318 precise measurements of the Temple. This is like the Torah's instructions on building the tabernacle—explicit and detailed to the point of monotony to let the reader know that this is a real thing he is describing. It is idealized in most respects, a perfect structure, as you would expect a visionary temple to be. Sometimes the numbers he writes down do not really make sense, as John Gill, an 18th-century Calvinist commentator observed. Gill wrote,

> [F]or that no material building can be designed is clear from this one observation; that not only the whole land of Israel would not be capable of having such a city as is here described built upon it, but even all Europe would not be sufficient; nor the whole world, according to the account of the dimensions which some give of it. The circumference of the city is said to be about eighteen thousand measures, Ezek 48:35; but what they are is not certain. Luther makes them to be thirty six thousand German miles; and a German mile being three of ours, the circuit of this city must be above a hundred thousand English miles; and this is sufficient to set aside all hypotheses of a material building, either of city or temple, the one being in proportion to the other.[1]

The perfectly square temple in the center of the perfectly square city is idealized, just as is the land distribution among the twelve tribes: all perfectly symmetrical. In chapter 48, Ezekiel only uses three numbers in laying out his plan for the city and the nation: five thousand, ten thousand, and twenty-five thousand. All in cubits. Either a length or a width. Like in a dream.

In contrast to the idealized structure are the matter-of-fact descriptions of the organization of the priests and the Temple worship. The Levites and priests in chapter 44 are real men Ezekiel is describing, not some heavenly band. And the holy days and the appointed feasts are not timeless. They are set according to our regular calendar. And the preparations for the sacrifices that Ezekiel sees according to the vision could almost be something right out of our Torah reading instead of our Haftarah reading. Ezekiel 45:17 says:

> It will be the duty of the prince to provide the burnt offerings, grain offerings and drink offerings at the festivals, the New Moons and the Sabbaths—at all the appointed festivals of Israel. He will provide the sin offerings, grain offerings, burnt offerings to make atonement for the Israelites.

This is a working temple—not a picture, not a model.

---

1. Gill, "Introduction to Ezekiel 40."

It is important to keep in mind two things about this prophecy in order to appreciate its full value. One, it is a prophecy from a Jew living in ancient Iraq, in Babylon. The Jewish homeland no longer existed as such. Solomon's Temple had been destroyed. The glory had departed. So one of the messages for Ezekiel in this vision is that God is not through with the Jews, not through with the Temple, not through with the land of Israel. Despite all appearances to the contrary. God is going to come back and it is going to be better than it ever was before. But still the same. The same Torah. The same *moedim*, the same festivals. The same worship and sacrifices. But better than ever.

A second message for Ezekiel is that God still has a place for him. Even after he has lost everything, God still has a plan and purpose for him. You see, Ezekiel was a priest without a temple to work in. He had been raised from childhood with this in mind, that he would grow up and serve God in his holy Temple. Then came the war. The invasion. The killings. The destruction. The exile. There was no place for a Jewish priest in ancient Iraq, by the waters of Babylon. His whole life had been devoted to one thing and one day it was all taken away. So, yes, those are priests he sees in his vision. Joy! It is no light matter for Ezekiel in exile to receive a word from the Lord, as in 44:15–16:

> But the Levitical priests, who are descendants of Zadok and who guarded my sanctuary when the Israelites went astray from me, are to come near to minister before me; they are to stand before me to offer sacrifices of fat and blood, declares the Sovereign LORD. They alone are to enter my sanctuary; they alone are to come near my table to minister before me and serve me as guards.

Free to Choose Torah

I think this is something the apostle Paul did not understand. That some Jews, even when they believe in Jesus as their savior, still want to observe the Torah, still want to worship as Jews, still want to be holy as Jews are instructed to be holy, still want to worship at the Temple, still want to make sacrifices to God. Even by the grace found in Yeshua HaMashiach. Messianic Jews want to circumcise their sons into the covenant of Abraham; want to keep Passover and remember our exodus from Egypt; want to hear the words of Torah read on Shabbat.

We are free to be ourselves in Messiah Yeshua. Even if it means worshipping on the seventh day instead of the first day of the week. Even if it means celebrating the Jewish holidays instead of Christmas and Easter. Even if it means bringing our children forward to read the Torah at their bat mitzvahs and bar mitzvahs instead of being baptized and confirmed in church. We are just that free.

So by this vision Ezekiel was set free from his personal despair, from his despondency, from his victimization, from his circumstances. God intended this salvation not only for him but for the nation in exile. There would be a future. There would be a future for the Jews. Like before, only better.

Today this vision of Ezekiel is described by some as the Third Temple. The hope it gave in the 6th century BC, when there was no temple, it now gives to some Jews, particularly the Orthodox, and some Christians, particularly conservative dispensationalists, who believe God plans another restoration of the Temple. Not all Jews and not all Christians agree that burnt offerings and animal sacrifices are to be hoped for any longer or that such a hope is relevant to our faith and practice as Jews, Christians, or Messianic Jews. I personally do not wait for the heavens to open and Jesus to descend from the clouds in a Second Coming, but I know some of us do. Related to that are biblical prophecies regarding the Temple. For me, no end-times orientation is given in this vision of Ezekiel's. Even though the Second Temple was destroyed by the Romans in 70 AD, I do not believe the glory ever departed from Israel. Whoever said that? But Ezekiel's is an idealized temple that fits well with expectations of an idealized future.

Who Is This?

I want to acknowledge the millennialist hopes that are attached to what Ezekiel saw without confining all the hope in this vision to the future. Because what I am really excited about is the portion of the vision that is our Haftarah reading today: Ezekiel 45:16—46:18. Here we read of a new character in the Hebrew Bible, a prince of Israel who performs the priestly sacrifices in the Temple. This is like what caused King Saul to lose his kingship, making a sacrifice at Gilgal instead of waiting for Samuel. When Samuel saw what he had done he told Saul his days as king were numbered because God wanted a man after his own heart (1 Sam 13). This is like what caused King Uzziah to be struck with leprosy, standing in the Temple holding a censer in his hand to burn incense unto the Lord, for which only a priest was consecrated (2 Chr 26).

Kings and princes do not make sacrifices. They do not serve God in the Temple. Except that is just what Ezekiel saw.

The Messianic Heavenly Vision   35

Who is this spiritual leader? Who is this princely priest, this priestly prince? What is this a vision of?

It is not really self-evident. Jewish scholars see the princely priest making the sacrifices described in Leviticus but certainly do not think that a vision of their sacrificial system would lead anyone to faith in Jesus, to faith in Yeshua as messiah. Christian scholars see the priestly prince ruling over the Temple and the nation but certainly do not think that a vision of the messiah would involve an idealized observance of sacrifices and the Jewish festivals.

Linking Torah observance together with Yeshua our messiah—or linking Christ Jesus to Torah observance—is just not something that many interpreters of the Bible have done for two thousand years. But here it is: a heavenly vision for Messianic Jews.

We see Yeshua, prophet, priest, and king, and we see the Torah: sin offerings, grain offerings, burnt offerings, and fellowship offerings to make atonement for the house of Israel. We see Yeshua leading us in our Torah observance: Ezekiel 45—46.

Not tomorrow. Not in some future millennium. Not post-rapture or pre-tribulation. But now. Today. In our own time. Here we are. The Messianic Jews, with a heavenly vision like Sha'ul's of Yeshua glorified. In our vision there is a city, a celestial city, but a geographical place as well. It is Jerusalem, the city of the great king. There is no temple there, only the wall of a temple. But we are not longing for one. We are not waiting for one in order to get started with the work God has for us to do on earth. Our heavenly vision is of Yeshua in the perfect temple in the perfect place with things in their perfect order. In our vision there is a river—a river whose streams "make glad the city of God, the holy place of the tabernacles of the most High" (Ps 46:4 KJV).

> God is in the midst of her; she shall not be moved:
> God shall help her, and that right early.
> The heathen raged, the kingdoms were moved: he uttered his
> voice, the earth melted.
> The LORD of hosts is with us; the God of Jacob is our refuge.
> (Ps 46:5–7 KJV; compare Ezek 47)

Ezekiel Foresaw a Torah-Observant Messiah

In our New Testament reading today, from the tenth chapter of the book of Hebrews, the writer uses a little Greek philosophy to say that the sacrifices of the book of Leviticus were only shadows of the true reality that was to come in Jesus Christ's sacrifice of his life from the cross. We respectfully disagree. We know that Torah observant Jews do not live in the shadows. They never have. God did not reach across time and space from heaven to create a chosen people provisionally. Partially. Temporarily. As shadows.

Yes, Jesus is the chosen one. Chosen by the same God who made a chosen people. These acts are not in conflict, as though forgiveness through Christ is the only forgiveness, as though prayer through Christ is the only prayer, as though obedience through Christ is the only obedience, as though election through Christ is the only election. That is not true. The witness of the Jews through time is the proof. The rise of Messianic Judaism in our time is the proof.

Ezekiel foresaw a messiah, the leader of Israel, making the same sacrifices, repeated endlessly, year after year, making perfect those who draw near to worship. One day he would come to earth and sacrifice himself and, from that altar on Calvary's hill, return to heaven. We see him there today, our messiah, our prince, our king.

Just as Ezekiel told us that a temple awaits us in heaven, and to place our hopes there, so we prepare ourselves for that day when we will meet Yeshua, face to face, our high priest who will lead us to the Father, our prince who is seated at the Father's right hand. We prepare ourselves for temple worship by remembering the Torah and remembering to keep its ways.

We expect the Father will be pleased.

4

A Way Through the Muddle

A Light is Dawning

With the zeal of a convert I have pursued God's calling. How to explain it? Any Jew who has heard of Messianic Judaism can tell you, of course, that Messianic Judaism is not Judaism. Any Christian who has heard of Messianic Judaism should be able to tell you, if they heard correctly, that Messianic Judaism is not a form of Christianity. Yet few Messianic Jews in the movement have been aggressive enough to declare that we are not part of the church. Instead, like my calling, this religion is a revelation: an act of God begun in the twentieth century that makes little sense to Jews or to Christians.

It is a light from heaven setting people free to practice Judaism with a messiah who is revealed in the gospels of the New Testament. This is true for Messianic Gentiles like me as it is for Messianic Jews like Rabbi Adam Yisroel. The legitimacy and integrity of this religion are bound up both in Jewish faith and practice and in worshipping the God of the New Testament. That this union can be authentic is the genius of Messianic Judaism.

For me, the great accomplishment of our movement has been discovering how to keep the Judaism in Messianic Judaism. Judaism came first, Christianity came second, and now Messianic Judaism has come third, a branch from both trees, miraculously enough. One definition of a miracle is something that no one sees coming. That fits Messianic Judaism. Another definition is something of supernatural origin, a revelation from above, whose authority rests in its origin with God. This is the standing Messianic Jews should claim in interfaith relations with Jews and Christians. We stand on our own, apart from the other biblical religions even as we have branched out from them.

From that perspective we must understand Judaism correctly if we are to understand Messianic Judaism. The popular understanding of Judaism is muddled in at least three ways. One way is to identify contemporary Jews with the Jews of the Bible. There are big differences. A second way is to see Jews as a racial-ethnic group identical to other ethnic groups according to conventional wisdom in a secular society. Faith's understanding of Jews as God's elect is instead more reliable and authentic. Thirdly, we are in the muddle if we claim that Jews are incomplete when they don't have Jesus. Yeshua's appearance was not a judgment upon Israel. And evangelizing to convert the chosen people is a logical and spiritual contradiction. Finding a way to come to terms with Jews regarding the sensitive subject of Jesus is a necessary task for believers in Messianic Judaism.

A Tricky Start

A good place to start building a foundation for a right relationship between Messianic Jews and Jews is at the muddle. Starting apart from the muddle would get people on board more quickly but then when the muddle appeared, as it would inevitably, its confusion would more quickly triumph. Traveling the road through the muddle with eyes open a pilgrim might discover that Messianic Judaism is neither confounding nor mistaken.

The muddle is made manifest by David B. Ruderman in his lecture "On Studying Jewish History." He discovers that contemporary Jews are hiding in plain sight, remarkable for their absence from the historical record. He states:

> Jewish history is seen from a traditional Christian perspective as a kind of prehistory of Christianity. What I mean by that: that the year 70 AD or CE, or 136—the destruction of the final Jewish community in Palestine, the final Roman revolt which was defeated, Jews were expelled, Israel was conquered by Rome and so on—in other words the period that follows Jesus's death and also the creation of the first Christian communities—at this point Jewish history more or less ends, from a Christian perspective.

> In other words Jews don't really have, at least for interest to Christians, a real political and cultural history. Jewish history ends with the rise of the Catholic church and this, of course, is the result of the rejection of Jesus by the rabbis, by the Jews themselves—we will define in another lecture the Pharisees, who they are and so on, and the later rabbis.
>
> In other words Jewish history is interesting as a prelude to Christianity. Jews were once the chosen people. They gave up their mantle of chosenness when the church assumed the right path. And the Jews continued stubbornly and awkwardly to go down their own path.
>
> Because the church is the true Israel what happens to Jews after the rise of Christianity is thus insignificant and not worthy of study.
>
> Now you may say this is too harsh. I mean, do people actually do that? But I must tell you: an essay written by the historian at Stanford, Gavin Langmuir, in the nineteen-sixties—when I was actually in graduate school—actually did a survey of, at that time, current Western historical texts: European history, world history, and so on. And indeed in these textbooks what you get is: Jews appear in the biblical period, then they disappear. Maybe you have a usurer, a money lender, walking around in the Middle Ages occasionally, here and there—a little anti-Semitism occasionally. Then you have the Holocaust and, some time, the rise of Israel. And nothing in between.
>
> In other words Jewish history pales in significance. It's not a conscious part.[1]

Professor Ruderman is giving voice to received wisdom and popular perception, in academia and in society. The dominant historical outlook does not to take note of the Jews over eons of time. The Jews have always been secondary to the Christians in Western society, and few outsiders have bothered to investigate their development through the centuries of the common era. What did they miss? Most Christians do not have a clue, as many Jews can attest.

Bible Study at the Synagogue

Michael Wex, in the first chapter of *Born to Kvetch: Yiddish Language and Culture in all its Moods*, points to this obfuscation from a different direction:

---

1. Ruderman, "On Studying Jewish History."

> Contrary to the usual "people of the book" shtik (the phrase, incidentally, comes from the Koran), Judaism is a Talmudic, not a biblical religion; without the interpretive guidance of the Talmud, the Hebrew Bible can lead to Jesus on the cross as easily as to me at my bar mitzvah. The Talmud is even called the Oral Torah and is considered to have been given to Moses along with the Written Torah. In the Jewish system of belief, you can't have one without the other: Judaism relates to the Bible *only* as it is refracted through the Talmud and Talmudic ways of thinking. Public-relations-minded anti-Semites who claim to dislike only "Talmudic" Jews are saying that they don't like any Jews: no Talmud, no Jews. It's like saying that they love everything about Christianity except for the skinny guy on the cross.[2]

The Talmud turns out to be the pivotal affirmation for outsiders to make in engaging Jews. Not reading it, necessarily, but adopting it as an assumption for Jewish identity and faith.

Many Christians seem to assume that Jews in America study the Old Testament the way Christians study the whole Bible: with an English translation while using commentaries. In their minds the chief differences are that Jews restrict themselves to the Old Testament, with a focus on the first five books of Moses, and basically use one commentary, the Talmud.

The truth is more like this. What if a Christian congregation today wanted to be just like the churches of the apostles in the first generation, as in Jerusalem or Damascus or Antioch as described in the book of Acts? Orthodox and Conservative Judaism carry into the present that kind of identification with their congregations from just that long ago, in those same regions. They exist in an unbroken chain of tradition going back to the origins of the Talmud in the second century AD.

So these Jews do not study the texts in translation. They study it in the original language of Hebrew. Of course many American Jews cannot read enough Hebrew to study with it; but any decent Torah study group will have a rabbi or a learned Jew who can lead the study accordingly.

An Analogy to the Gospels

Moreover Jews study the Hebrew Bible with an authoritative interpretation to guide their understanding. The Talmud is not a commentary in the way of other biblical commentaries. It is more like what the teaching of Jesus was to those first Christians. Jesus was not giving commentary. He spoke with

---

2. Wex, *Born to Kvetch*, 13–14.

authority. By analogy the Talmud is a comparable authority. It is the Oral Torah, alongside the Written Torah.

Interestingly, parts of the Talmud were being written by Jewish rabbis at the same time and in the same regions as Christian teachers were writing the gospels and the other books of the New Testament. This Jewish history is in *The Talmud: A Biography* by Harry Freedman as well as in Professor Ruderman's lectures.

If a church today wanted to be truly apostolic it would not use the Bible because the churches of the apostles met before it had been assembled. This is a silly idea, of course. Every Christian church today has evolved from first century, first-generation Christianity (the proto-orthodox part) and has inherited the New Testament as sacred scripture. Similarly Judaism has evolved from that first century and has inherited the Talmud as sacred scripture. As David Ruderman and Michael Wex observe, intelligent people both religious and secular don't recognize this, don't get this, and don't want to know about this. For most Christians and for many non-Jewish intellectuals, the Jews of the Bible are the Jews. The reality is too confusing to bother with. Better to stick with the muddle of outdated perceptions than listen to another voice outside the Bible's.

Unless you want to be a Messianic Jew. Then you want to get the history right because you are a new branch on a tree of religion which is both Jewish and Christian. Jews, from their perspective, do not recognize that relationship. Christians, from their perspective, misunderstand that relationship. But we are not like the Church of Jesus Christ of the Latter-day Saints (the Mormons) who published a new book of revelation as the authoritative interpretation of the Bible. Messianic Judaism has nothing new to offer other than a new and different understanding of what is taught in the Bible. We are not the Jews, and we are not the Christians, but we also are a biblical faith. We are the third biblical religion.

But we are not Talmudic Jews. Michael Wex says that is the only kind of Jew there is. We beg to differ. To do that you have to know that all Jews are Talmudic and that the Christians don't know this. First, grasp that the Jewish religious authority is not simply the Old Testament. Second, grasp that Messianic Jews do not share this reliance upon the Talmud's authority. Finally, perceive that Messianic Jews are unique in combining the authority of the Torah with the authority of the New Testament. This is different from other Jews who combine the authority of the Torah with the authority of the Talmud. This is also different from Christians who qualify the authority of the Torah and Old Testament with the greater authority of the New Testament and, in some cases, with the authority of church teaching.

Messianic Jews are not misguided Christians. Nor are they Jews like other Jews.

A Jewish Soul is Unique

This brings us to the age-old question, What is a Jew? The answer can be found if you know where to look. It can be found today in Hebron. Tuvia Tenenbom was the one who went there to look and he published the answer in his 2015 memoir *Catch the Jew!*:

> I am invited to a Jewish family, religious like all of them here, for a Shabbat meal, the first of three meals in the next twenty-four hours that religious families celebrate together every Sabbath.
>
> And we talk. Parents, children, and friends of children. I want them to explain to me what it means to be Jewish. I ask it because I changed from a Jew to a non-Jew, or vice-versa, in a matter of minutes just moments ago.
>
> They respond by saying that a Jew is a unique being, a preferred being, a chosen being, a being born with a "Jewish soul."
>
> Isn't this, more or less, in line with Adolf Hitler's idea of a German? You don't tell a Jew, whatever "Jew" means, that he or she is a Hitlerite and expect them to agree with you. The people sitting at this Shabbat table think that I have lost my mind or, better yet, that I'm a psychotic leftist.
>
> Truth is, and I must admit, there's one huge difference between them and Adolf. If I told Adolf Hitler that he's just like the settlers of Hebron, a right-wing Jew, I don't think he would have continued to feed me. Adolf would have fed me to the animals, but here I get fed some animals: excellent chicken, for example. I eat the chicken as I keep pushing my hosts to the edge and they tell me to eat more.
>
> That's a difference. Yes.
>
> But I stick to my guns and keep on asking for answers. The Jew, they finally react to my earlier question, doesn't have different blood, as Hitler said about his Aryan friends, but a different soul.
>
> What the heck are you talking about?
>
> "Every human being has a soul. Don't you know that?"
>
> Jewish and non-Jewish?
>
> "Yes, of course."
>
> And the non-Jewish soul is like that of animals, let's say dogs, but the Jewish soul is Godly. Right?

"We didn't say that. We said that the Jews, by God's design, have a different soul."

Sorry. What does this mean?

"If you don't know what a soul is, there's nothing to talk about."

Well, maybe you could explain to me.

"A soul, you don't know what it is?"

Honestly, I don't.

This creates a new discussion, esoteric in language, absurd in thought, and totally incomprehensible to me. I hear words flying around the table and I have no clue to their meaning. In short: I'm lost.

I tell them: Could you please stop hovering above reality and start communicating with me via the use of human communication?

"Try the chocolate cake," they suggest.

I do. It's delicious.

"This is the best Shabbat meal we ever had," my hosts' son announces to the assembly, and profusely thanks me for challenging them. "We will not forget this evening and it will make us think," he declares, gratefully shaking hands with me.[3]

Tuvia Tenenbom has never heard of the Jewish soul but his host family knows about it. These people are Jews by birth. It is in birth that we are ensouled, that we receive our soul, that we have a soul. A Jewish soul is unique from every other. It follows then that a convert to Judaism is Jewish without having a Jewish soul. The distinction between having a Jewish soul and being Jewish in a religious sense is an important one. This is particularly true for Messianic Jews, who claim a Jewish soul apart from the Talmudic Jewish religion. The great idea of Messianic Judaism is that you can follow the way of Jesus as taught in the New Testament with a Jewish soul and not lose it, even when you receive Jesus as messiah.

Redefining The Christ

Now we are dealing with two important distinctions, two important truths. They are both central to the faith and practice of Messianic Judaism. One is the distinction between being a Jew and belonging to the Jewish religion. The other is the distinction between receiving Jesus as a messiah and receiving, in a Christian sense, Jesus as the Messiah or Christ. For Christians there is only one Christ, one Messiah. Messiah is capitalized in Christianity and

3. Tenenbom, *Catch the Jew!*, 113–14.

is always preceded in English by the article "the." But it is not in the Hebrew scriptures of the Bible. In Hebrew the term is neither capitalized nor preceded by an article, and so it is just as accurately translated "a messiah" as "the Messiah." Compare the NASB and NRSV translations of Dan. 9:25, the former with the title capitalized ("Messiah the Prince"), the latter with lower case letters ("an anointed prince").

The difference is simply this: the Messiah, being the one and only, can be defined once and for all, and the church and writers of the New Testament have, once and for all, defined the Messiah as divine, as the incarnation of God. That is Christianity. Believing this way makes one a Christian.

On the other hand, a messiah, like a king, is an anointed human being in the Hebrew lexicon. Cyrus, king of Persia, was certainly one of us, and in Isaiah 45:1 he is given the title "his anointed," translated into the Greek Septuagint as *christos*, a title which is capitalized when transliterated as "Christ" only when it applies to Jesus in the New Testament. But there are many other anointed ones in the Bible who are, of course, not divinities.

Learning to be Selective

Messianic Jews and Gentiles with a Jewish monotheism adore Yeshua. We love Jesus. We obey Jesus. We surrender ourselves to Jesus. This sounds like we are Christians who worship Jesus but we draw the line in a different way and do not go as far as the high Christology found in the prologue to the Gospel of John; and we do not go as far as interpreting as incarnational the verse "that God was reconciling the world to himself in Christ" (2 Cor 5:19). We are not trinitarian. Still we are in Christ as part of his covenant. Being "in Christ" (2 Cor 5:17) and being "in Isaac" (Gen 21:12 KJV) is a both/and possibility, not either/or.

So there are some verses in the New Testament that we hedge on, or that we pass over, even as we embrace the New Testament as sacred and authoritative scripture. In this practice we follow in the way of the apostles, of the writers of the New Testament, and of the church fathers who equivocated upon and passed over verses in the Hebrew scriptures which offended and contradicted their Christian teaching. They co-opted another religion's sacred book for their own purposes and had it both ways when necessary; as in adopting Psalm 23, which concludes with the affirmation, "and I will dwell in the house of the LORD forever," without reference to the atonement of Jesus Christ or baptism or being born again.

A prime example of the selectivity of Christian readers of the Old Testament is lifting up from its pages tithing as a religious obligation. But tithing is no more a duty in the Hebrew scriptures than is keeping kosher and not eating bacon and eggs or, as interpreted by the Talmud, a cheeseburger. One of the most sacred duties in the Old Testament is keeping the Sabbath. Christian readers ignore the verses on the Mosaic regulation of the seventh day of the week.

That is Christianity, a religion of its own. Messianic Jews and Gentiles ask for the same understanding. We are a religion using the Hebrew Bible and the New Testament as sacred scriptures without being bound to Christian doctrine or Talmudic authority.

A Dialogue

I hear Jewish wise men and scholars doubting.
   "More than one Judaism? How could this be?"
You have got to be kidding. What has Hollywood to do with Brooklyn? What has Ethiopia to do with Tel Aviv? What have the Orthodox to do with the Reconstructionists?
   "Not Jesus, that's for certain."
I pulled these quotes from *Basic Judaism* by Milton Steinberg:

> For—and this is the crux of the matter—Judaism is an organism; the fabric of its weaving is alive.[4]

> Judaism exhibits a unified and continuing spiritual pattern throughout its history. Except for its beginnings at one extreme and its most recent phases at the other.[5]

> The Tradition holds then that the world's redemption is to be effected by a single man in one climactic episode. About this basic faith the Jewish spirit has woven variants innumerable.[6]

So Judaism can be flexible, evolving over time with innumerable variants woven into its fabric. Could this be the time for one more variety? I argue there is much in common—even the Jewish soul—between Messianic Judaism and Judaism. I do not speak for the evangelical Messianic Jews who insist on Christian beliefs. Can we make a distinction between them and Messianic Jews who are strict monotheists, especially as that applies to Jesus?

---

4. Steinberg, *Basic Judaism*, 4.
5. Steinberg, *Basic Judaism*, 9.
6. Steinberg, *Basic Judaism*, 168.

A Parable

I am inspired further by Milton Steinberg to press my argument with this illustration from *Basic Judaism*.

> In medieval Jewish literature there is to be found an exquisite and illuminating parable which, with the slightest adaptation, is admirably suited to stand for everything this book has tried to say.
>
> Once, we are told, a traveler making his way through a difficult and perilous countryside came to the bank of a river too deep to be forded. Return he could not, nor remain where he was. How, then, was he to come to the other side? Then he bethought himself of the purse which dangled from his girdle, containing in the form of gold pieces all his worldly wealth. In the extremity of his need he began to toss the coins one by one into the river, hoping so to raise a pathway for himself over its bed.
>
> In vain! The bag emptied; the river still could not be crossed.
>
> Finally one gold piece remained. Holding this in his hand, the traveler cast about for some other device. Looking here and there he espied a ferry boat far down the river which in his frenzy he had failed to notice earlier. Regretting that he had wasted his treasure to no purpose, yet fortunate in that one coin was left to him for passage money, he hastened to the boat, gave the gold piece to the ferryman and crossed to the other side, so saving his life and going on his way.[7]

A Christian story would have Jesus carry the traveler across the river on his back, sacrificing his life in the doing of it. A Messianic Jewish story stays with this version, with the slightest adaptation. In our story the ferryman is Jesus.

It is not the same story as it was told. And Messianic Judaism is not Judaism. We agree that adherents to both faiths cross the river and on this boat. When you judge that a Messianic Jew stops being a Jew if his ferryman is Jesus, we beg to differ.

"So how could there be two ferrymen, one for all Jews and another for Messianic Jews? The story has one ferry boat. Is the ferryman of Judaism simply the Messianic Jesus in disguise, saving everyone after all? If so, what do you take us for?"

What if we promise not to think that, not to suppose that, and promise not to talk to Jews about a ferryman. What if our slightest adaptation also has a machine that takes gold coins, and you simply put your gold coin into

---

7. Steinberg, *Basic Judaism*, 171.

the slot, the ferry starts up and takes you across the river, and you meet no one on the boat. It is just you and all the other Jews on one big boat.

"Now you are changing the story again. We give you an inch, you take a mile. You put all the Jews on one boat, and it is bound to start leaking. You want our Torah but not our Talmud? Better that you should learn to be Jewish and never learn Hebrew. You are a pious fraud."

How about this? The same story with an addendum. We are another traveler, a second traveler. We too are down to one gold coin, standing on the same river bank, in the same situation, but later in time. And, in our frenzy, we too espy a ferry boat far down the river. This one is just like the first, except the ferryman is Jesus. So there could be two ferrymen if there were two crossings separated by such a flimsy thing as time. And the boats belong to the same fleet. You wouldn't sink our boat, would you?

"Your ferryman is a tricky fellow. If he swims he will probably jump your ship and swim over to ours, asking to get on board. And some of us, being Jews, would let him on. And that would be the end of our tradition, the end of our religion, and the end of our people."

Without End

Don't look here and see Haman the Agagite once again. Nothing, no one, no way, no how, can bring an end to the existence of Jewish souls. If every Jew converted to Messianic Judaism it would be the end of Judaism and, according to the Talmud, the end of the world. May it never be so. Messianic Judaism is a religion, not the religion. We are not exclusive in the way many Christian traditions are. We are one boat crossing the river of life, appreciative of the other boats making the same journey, and very much like the boat carrying the Jewish souls exclusively. The ferryman we follow is also this way.

This book tells how this could be. You may not care to ever meet this messiah. But we are a growing presence in the world, and we believe God is with us in both our allegiance to Yeshua and in our Torah observance. Wouldn't it be just like God to get the goyim observing Torah after the Holocaust? Don't be a curmudgeon. Some good may yet come of it, even for the Jews.

5

The Jewish Soul and the Holy Spirit

The ideas of having a soul and of losing your soul are spiritual and sacred. It is possible to live one's whole life long and never get around to considering spiritual and sacred matters, but for Jews they are a birthright that almost has to be turned away from if not acknowledged and embraced. Abraham Joshua Heschel articulated the assumptions of having a Jewish soul in an essay he wrote for the inaugural edition (1951) of *Zionist Quarterly*, a journal of the Zionist Organization of America that had been instrumental in gathering support for the formation of the state of Israel in 1948.[1] Rabbi Heschel entitled his contribution, "To Be a Jew. What Is It?"
It is:

> conveying the taste of eternity in our daily living.[2]

It is to live in response to God:

> Our souls tremble with the echo of unforgettable experiences and the sublime expectation of our own response.[3]

It is to make a correspondence from within to without:

---

1. Zionist Organization of America, "Fighting for Israel."
2. Heschel, "To Be a Jew," 4.
3. Heschel, "To Be a Jew," 5.

> In exposing ourselves to God we discover the divine in ourselves and its correspondence to the divine beyond ourselves.[4]

More than correspondence, there exists a kinship between the Jewish soul and God:

> Israel is a spiritual order in which the human and the ultimate, the natural and the holy enter a lasting covenant, in which kinship with God is not an aspiration but a reality of destiny.[5]

Finally, it is an assignment, a mission, a duty:

> We are God's stake in human history.[6]

And:

> We carry the gold of God in our souls to forge the gate of the kingdom.[7]

These are the assumptions of Judaism. They cannot be deduced from the facts, they cannot be demonstrated from the historical record, they cannot be proven from the evidence. Just as every soul goes undetected in the human anatomy, so the spiritual and sacred identity of a Jew is hidden from the world. But it is real. God works through Jews by a secret, hidden choice. Do not assume otherwise.

Existential and Metaphysical Leaping

In every human being is hidden a soul, but the Jewish soul is particular and peculiar in its spiritual capacity for wrestling with God and others. Messianic Judaism only makes sense when it owns this distinction and has it recognized by other Jews. Jewish identity is at stake. This passage from an Orthodox Jewish writer, Yitzchak Rubin, is instructive about what that purpose entails. From the title of his essay, "What was G-d's purpose in creating man?" it is not clear he intends to distinguish the Jewish soul from others. But he does:

> It is impossible to understand the vast mystery of G-d's will, but seeing the greatness of spirit that is humanly possible in others, one can gain a glimpse of the aching drive that is in our holy

---

4. Heschel, "To Be a Jew," 5.
5. Heschel, "To Be a Jew," 7.
6. Heschel, "To Be a Jew," 11.
7. Heschel, "To Be a Jew," 11.

essence. This world is G-d's way of giving our souls the possibility of greatness—unfortunately this comes with the possibility to do the opposite as well.

The Kotzker Rebbe was once asked how it is possible for us to persevere in this material world; how can a soul prosper in a physical world full of the magnetism of the mundane? He answered with a lovely analogy: G-d sends a soul down to earth on a ladder. He then takes the ladder away and calls out for the soul to climb back up to its celestial source. Some souls give up right away: "How can I get back to G-d? He has taken away the ladder." Others try a bit, they leap up doing a few mitzvoth, but soon they too tire, "After all, G-d has taken away the ladder." Then there are the wise souls; they say, "If G-d took away the ladder yet he calls me to reach up, then, although it seems impossible, that must not be my concern. I must leap and leap and leap again doing G-d's will, for that is what He expects of me."

G-d wants us to leap and leap ever closer to our source, and although it may seem impossible, it doesn't mean we are not meant to do so anyway. That is why our souls were sent here in the first place, and the entire creation is meant to facilitate this.[8]

God has a purpose on earth that can only be accomplished by Jewish souls. Messianic Jews are shouting out, "That's us too." The Jewish soul has this capacity to carry on in the face of deprivation and absurdity and unrealistic expectations by God. The chosen people are equipped existentially and metaphysically for the mission peculiar to them. Director Helen Hunt also pictures a Jewish soul in her 2007 movie, *Then She Found Me*, dramatizing "a glimpse of the aching drive that is in our holy essence."[9]

The seeming folly of the idea that Jews are different from non-Jews in their souls comes with the blessing of being a Jew. No one can communicate it in the world without sounding odd. But it is a fundamental assumption of Judaism that Messianic Jews share. Their success has been limited by their inability to persuade other Jews that they have not lost their Jewish soul through apostasy or assimilation.

Always Jewish, Absolutely Not the Church

None of this talk of souls is commonplace. The generic terms of psychology and spirituality register but there are no reports in the media, academia or popular discourse about having a soul, losing your soul, or distinguishing

---

8. Rubin, "What was G-d's purpose," 91.
9. *Then She Found Me*, directed by Hunt.

between types of souls. But the soul can be found in the assumption that "What is it to be a Jew?" is a profound question. It is hidden in Messianic Judaism's struggle to define itself.

Paul Liberman was a pioneer in the Messianic movement, as he describes in his memoir *Don't Call Me Christian*. Observe in this passage the absolute distinction between Jewish and non-Jewish he is intent on maintaining:

> Almost as soon as Beth Messiah began to hold meetings on May 18, 1973, I realized I would be required to "explain" our purpose to the outside Jewish community. I needed to be able to honestly profess that we were not an appendage, subsidiary, affiliate, or offshoot of any Christian (Gentile) denomination or ministry. We were a Jewish congregation and always would be. We absolutely were *not* a "church." For this reason, if we identified as "*Beth Messiah, a Messianic Synagogue*" immediately followed by, "*affiliated with the Hebrew Christian Alliance of America*," it would seem an inherent contradiction in our stated goal. How could you have a "Christian synagogue?" It was an oxymoron! For me that was a major problem.[10]

Paul Liberman and I want to lift the Jewish soul out of the traditional Jewish context and put it in a new Messianic context. How could believers in Messiah Yeshua of the New Testament remain Jews? Traditionally that has been perceived as violating the Jewish soul and identity.

Meeting the Messianic Jewish Challenge

This is forcefully articulated in a document originated by the Jewish Community Relations Council of New York (JCRCNY) entitled, "Meeting the Challenge: Hebrew Christians and the Jewish Community." It is their answer to the question "What is it to be a Jew?" They know the truth for themselves. They know it in their souls. Outside of themselves the Jewish soul cannot exist. The executive summary of the 1993 paper was on their webpage for many years but has reappeared as an article on the Jews for Judaism website. It illustrates the conflict Messianic Jews face from their own people who hold that the Christian break from Judaism was complete and cannot be bridged by "new Jewish Christian views." Traditional boundaries protect the integrity and reality of Judaism:

---

10. Liberman, *Don't Call Me Christian*, 214.

> From its inception, Judaism has had specific regulations which define membership for individuals and has set limits beyond which one is considered as having left the Jewish community. For organizations, standards have also been set for inclusion within the Jewish communal structure. Even though those members of Hebrew Christian or Messianic Jewish groups who are originally of Jewish status retain their ability to pass on this Jewish status to their offspring, they face a significant loss of privileges within the Jewish community, including denial of membership in synagogues and other Jewish communal organizations, and denial of immediate Israeli citizenship under the Law of Return.
>
> The Jewish messianic idea differs significantly from the Christian one. According to Jewish tradition the Messiah will not be divine or change the Jewish obligation to observe the Torah.[11]

Here are criteria for overcoming the fundamental handicap of a Messianic Judaism that insists on an evangelical identity. On the one hand, the contradiction in the idea of a God-man is common knowledge and common sense. On the other hand, it is a revelation from God that Messianic Jews can now embrace a human messiah in the pages of the gospels. The Christian messianic idea is exclusivistic as well as incarnational. It excludes traditional Talmudic Jews. The JCRCNY and Jews for Judaism cannot reason with evangelical Jews:

> For all the above reasons, Hebrew Christianity is not a form of Judaism and its members, even if they are of Jewish birth, cannot be considered members of the Jewish community. Hebrew Christians are in radical conflict with the communal interests and the destiny of the Jewish people. They have crossed an unbreachable chasm by accepting another religion....
>
> Historically, the belief in or practice of any other religious tradition has been understood to lead to the loss of rights to full participation in the Jewish community, which has the following ramifications:
>
> - denial of membership or honors in synagogal and/or Jewish communal organizations
> - exclusion from burial in Jewish cemeteries
> - refusal of Jewish communal funds to support any activities of Hebrew Christians or Messianic Jewish groups

---

11. Jews for Judaism, "Meeting the Challenge," sections 2–3.

- exclusion from access to Jewish communal facilities or mailing lists.[12]

What are the JCRCNY and Jews for Judaism defending? It is not just tribal identity in the way other racial-ethnic groups guard their membership. There is more at stake here than customary boundary disputes between insiders and outsiders, between belonging to your people and assimilating with others. What makes these Jewish taboos so strict is the spiritual nature of Jewish identity. Compromising that identity can be a matter of losing your Jewish soul.

What I am asking for is a miracle: to belong to another religion and take your Jewish soul with you. Jews want to preserve their identity from the threats of genocide, assimilation and apostasy. These are the dangers in this world to the Jewish soul, the gold of God. Conversion to another religion can be apostasy or assimilation. For the past fifty years, Messianic Jews have proven that while they are not Talmudic Jews, neither are they apostates or assimilated. They have kept their Jewish souls. They want to keep as well their ancestral ties and identity.

An Appeal to Kinship

The Messianic Jewish ministry of Hashivenu, in "A Vision for a Maturing Messianic Judaism," makes this appeal within their Core Value #1. They are born Jews, and they know that, for them, taking up the New Testament has not been an abandonment of being Jewish:

> Instead, being "Jewish" is, for us, a fundamental religious category. We are those who by birth share in the covenant God made with Abraham, Isaac, and Jacob, and whose ancestors pledged themselves and their descendants to a particular way of life with God at Sinai. Having been born into the covenant, we have also come to recognize Messiah Yeshua as the One sent by God to bring the covenant to its appointed goal.[13]

"The covenant" applies to all Jews, so why not them? They appeal to the idea of a variety of Judaisms:

12. Jews for Judaism, "Meeting the Challenge," section 5.
13. Hashivenu, "Core Value #1."

> We recognize our kinship with other Judaisms and believe that we have much of profound importance to learn from them, as well as something vitally important to share with them.[14]

This is a different expression of the ferryman appeal I made in chapter 4. Both are over boundary disputes. Hashivenu claims that their recognition of Messiah Yeshua does not create a boundary between Jews and Messianic Jews. It is overridden by the common birthright. My ferryman appeal recognizes Messiah Yeshua as a man among men, as every Jewish messiah has been, eliminating the Jesus boundary between Jews and Messianic Jews.

Another Way of Seeing

The companion truth to Messianic Jews keeping their Jewish souls instead of losing them by apostasy or assimilation is the truth that evangelical Christianity is in error when it denies the validity and integrity of Judaism. This recognition approaches the conflict from the other side of the boundary between Christians and Jews.

The unique identity of the Jews as God's chosen people is not a minority opinion within Judaism or in large parts of the church, including Roman Catholicism. The Presbyterian Church (USA)'s statement, "A Theological Understanding of the Relationship Between Christians and Jews," bolsters its affirmation of the validity of Judaism by listing similar statements from across the church:

> Since World War II, statements and study documents dealing with Jewish-Christian relations have been issued by a number of churches and Christian bodies. Among these are the Vatican's Nostra Aetate (1965), the Report of the Faith and Order Commission of the World Council of Churches (1968), the statement of the Synod of the Reformed Church of Holland (1970), the statement of the French Bishops' Committee for Relations with the Jews (1973), the report of the Lutheran World Federation (1975), the statement of the Synod of Rhineland Church in West Germany (1980), the report of the Christian/Jewish Consultation Group of the Church of Scotland (1985), and the study of the World Alliance of Reformed Churches (1986).[15]

The idea that God hears the prayer of a Jew is a commonplace in most churches and denominations. That is, the idea that there are unsaved Jews

---

14. Hashivenu, "Core Value #1."
15. Office of the General Assembly, "A Theological Understanding," 3.

who need to receive Yeshua in order to find God is a false idea in light of the chosenness of the Jewish people, in light of the covenant relationships that are every Jew's birthright, and in light of the unique value of the Jewish soul.

The Charismatic Influence

Messianic Jews created a bind for themselves at the start of their movement in the 1970s when they identified with evangelical Protestantism and its emphasis on being saved through a conversion experience of coming to Christ (the Messiah). Paul Liberman describes in detail his baptism in the Holy Spirit, the consequent gift of speaking in tongues, and the initial evangelistic efforts in 1972 with another Jewish believer, Sid Roth, who was part of an established Pentecostal ministry, the Full Gospel Business Men's Fellowship.[16] Carol Harris-Shapiro connects the origins of the Messianic movement with the charismatic renewal movements in the late sixties and early seventies. It touched a rising generation of believers who were sometimes labeled "the Jesus people." The connection is informal but revealing:

> One of these new groups was the Jesus people, a loosely connected group of young people who combined fundamentalism and a dedication to evangelism with a counterculturalstyle (Lipson 1990). Many of the Jesus people also practiced Spirit-filled or Charismatic Christianity, a form of Christian belief and worship that believes the New Testament "gifts of the Spirit" can be exercised today, such as healing the sick through prayer, speaking in tongues, and receiving direct prophecies from God.[17]

I have worshipped with four Messianic congregations, and three of them practice the gifts of the Spirit in mostly personal, private ways. At the MJAA Conference in 2018, there were prayers for healing, and I witnessed one woman slain in the Spirit after asking for the laying on of hands at the end of the evening service. The evidence of the charismatic side of Messianic Judaism is anecdotal, but if it has influenced the growth of the movement, this would explain a lot. As Paul Liberman discovered, the baptism of the Holy Spirit is self-validating. It is its own source of authority. It is an experience of God that is self-confirming. No one on earth can deny the truth of someone else's spiritual experience.

---

16. Liberman, *Don't Call Me Christian*, 158–61.
17. Harris-Shapiro, *Messianic Judaism*, 24–25.

Divorce and Remarriage

My idea would be to distinguish Messianic Judaism from the fundamentalism and evangelicalism to which it was initially and enduringly connected. Consider Blaise Pascal's observation that in the New Testament era the baptism of the Holy Spirit was cited as evidence for excluding Jewishness from the church:

> When St. Peter and the Apostles discussed abolishing circumcision, where it was a question of going against the law of God, they did not look to the prophets but simply to the reception of the Holy Spirit in the person of the uncircumcised.
>
> They judged it more certain that God approved those whom he fills with his spirit than that the law must be observed.
>
> They knew that the only purpose of the law was the Holy Spirit, and that since He could certainly be received without circumcision, this was not necessary.[18]

In the Messianic movement the appearance of the gifts of the Spirit may have also been experienced as confirmation of the assumptions of Protestant evangelicalism with its high Christology, trinitarian doctrine, and emphasis on evangelizing the Jews (and other non-believers). I am claiming that it can also be received as the birth pangs of a new religion, a third biblical religion that has different assumptions than the Full Gospel Business Men and other conservative Protestant ministries. We are not Christians. And we are not a branch of Judaism. But we are Spirit-born and Spirit-led and Spirit-saved. Take it to prayer: King Jesus was a man. God made another covenant through him. With that unique Jewish soul, the Messianic Jews and their Messianic movement are now one way God is redeeming the world. We have gifts and perspective that belong to no one else.

---

18. Pascal, *Pensees*, 135.

Discussion B:
Believing as Gentiles and as Jews

Read 1 Corinthians 1:30.

John Calvin, a Reformed theologian, explains this verse this way:

> Paul here ascribes to Christ four titles that sum up all this excellence and every benefit that we receive from him.
>
> First it is said that Christ is made "our wisdom," by which Paul means that we receive in him perfect wisdom, because the Father has fully revealed himself to us in Christ, so that we may not desire to know anything else except Christ. . . .
>
> Second, Paul says that Christ is "our righteousness." This means that we are acceptable to God through Christ, because Christ atoned for our sins by his death, and his obedience is credited to us as righteousness. The righteousness of faith consists in the remission of sins and acceptance through God's grace, and it is through Christ that we obtain both.
>
> Third, Paul calls Christ our sanctification, by which he means that even though we are unholy by nature, we are renewed by the Spirit of Christ for holiness, so that we may serve God. From this we learn that it is impossible for us to be justified freely by faith alone without at the same time leading holy lives. . . .
>
> Fourth, Paul teaches us that Christ is given to us for redemption, by which he means that through Christ's goodness we are freed from all bondage to sin and from all the misery that results from it.[1]

---

1. Calvin, "Christ's Titles," 42–43.

This is the normative Christian experience and the normative Messianic Jewish experience. Christians achieve it in one movement of being "in Christ Jesus." Paul says it is accomplished by God—"It is because of him that you are in Christ Jesus"(1 Cor 1:30). Calvin says it is accompanied by faith. The movement is transactional. It involves a transaction: a deal, an exchange, a compact. Once we were lost, now we are found.

Messianic Jews achieve it in a double movement of being "in Christ Jesus." Messianic Jews, on the basis of being Jews, are the chosen people of God even as they come to make a decision about Yeshua, about sin and salvation. Jews are born into the world as part of a covenant. Do they lose that covenant through sin, through evil, through killing Bathsheba's husband, or through killing the Messiah? In Romans 9:1–18, Paul says that they may. They may be hardened (9:18). But first they are Jewish. Before they lose their covenant status they are born into the world with it. As Abraham Joshua Heschel says, you cannot stop being a Jew: "We are Jews as we are men."[2]

The Double Movement to Faith and Salvation

So the first defining movement for a Jew to be in Yeshua the Messiah is to embrace his or her Jewishness, his or her covenant through Abraham and Moses and David. Messianic Jews do not come to the judgment seat of Christ as strangers like everyone else. Messianic Jews sin as Jews, are lost as Jews, repent as Jews, and believe in Yeshua as Jews. The second defining movement performed by God brings this Jew "into" Christ Jesus, "into" Messiah Yeshua. The experience for Jews must be a double movement.

That second movement is what Calvin describes, which is the experience of the justification and sanctification that belongs to everyone who receives Yeshua as their Savior. Messianic Jews received a renewed covenant when they are brought into relationship with God through Yeshua. Christians receive a new covenant. One is a double movement, the other is single. The grace of God is experienced differently according to the different histories.

The Mother Tongue has Significance

Think of it in terms of baggage. Jews have Hebrew baggage. That is, Hebrew is their mother tongue; their first language. No one else has this particular

---

2. Heschel, "Mission to the Jews," 110.

baggage. No one else knows what *hesed* means because *hesed* is a Hebrew word that cannot be adequately translated into any other language. But Jews get *hesed* as their birthright because it is a word in their mother tongue. English speakers make due with "lovingkindness" or "loyalty" or "goodness" as translations of *hesed* but they are all only partially representative.

In reverse, there are Greek words in the New Testament that cannot be translated into Hebrew. There is no single Hebrew word precisely equivalent to *charis*, commonly translated in English as "grace." Jews do not have a phrase for "the grace of God." There is no evidence that Yeshua knew the word.

Now French speakers may want to relate their translation inadequacies to my argument, but they are not the same. The biblical revelation of God was not given in French, so there is no prior track of religious significance laid down in the French vocabulary. When you learn Psalm 23 in French, you get the meaning of *hesed* in verse 6 by interpreting the Hebrew revelation in the best translation. "*Charis*" in French is likewise no obstacle because French words have no intrinsic sacred meanings for Christians that would confuse a translation from Greek.

When you have a first language filled with religious significance, it is difficult to convey the truths of another religion written in a second language. So, to grasp the reality of Yeshua which was given in Greek, the Messianic Jew has to make a double movement: first, stop thinking like a Jew and, second, take hold of the revelation on its non-Hebraic terms. Then discover grace. The Christian believer gets the revelation, in Greek or in translation, in a single movement. God did not already reveal himself in any other mother tongue.

The Means to a New Reality

In one way, the double movement is into Jewishness on the way to receiving Yeshua as messiah. In another way, the double movement is out of the Hebrew language on the way to receiving the gospel (another word that does not translate into Hebrew). The genius and gift of Messianic Judaism, then, is coming back into a Hebraic mindset with the gospel. A third movement. What was once an obstacle, Hebrew baggage, is the means to a new reality. A new religion. It is accomplished by the grace of God.

Questions

1. Do you object to the idea that, as a Messianic Jew, you stopped thinking in Hebrew in order to grasp the New Testament revelation of Yeshua? If so, say a bit about your reading of the first chapter of 1 Corinthians. A rabbinic Jew would find it strange. It is scripture, not just any letter, but there is nothing remotely like it in the Hebrew Bible. Name some of the ways the Old Testament and the New Testament are different.

2. How does embracing one's Jewishness as the first movement in conversion to faith in Yeshua a messiah differ from the idea of becoming a completed Jew?

3. *Hesed* is a Jewish birthright. What other words or ideas are so Jewish that they cannot really be translated or carried over to another language or culture?

6

Commentary on Romans 9, 10, and 11

The Question at the Heart of the Matter

> In a famous article, Krister Stendahl argued that generations of scholars have read into Paul, and Romans, a modern preoccupation with the individual that is simply not present in Paul's day. Luther's question was, "How can a sinner get right with a wrathful God?" But that is not Paul's question. Typical of the corporate way of thinking at that time, he wants to answer the question: "How can Jews and Gentiles cohere in one people of God?"[1]

This question can be a basis for validating Messianic Judaism and its soteriology. It reflects my experience. But the revelation of Messianic Judaism I have received is not about the Jews being hardened by God (Rom 11:7–8). Paul's dilemma arises from limiting himself to two choices: the Jews or the saved in Christ. He proceeds to collapse the two into a vision of one work of God, one olive tree, one salvation for all (11:26). Messianic Judaism relies upon on the diversity in God's election and the variety in his means of grace. Because it displaces neither Judaism or Christianity, it instead asks to be

---

1. Moo, *Romans*, 25.

a new answer to the question, "How can Jews and Gentiles cohere as one people of God?"

> Stendahl's general approach has been widely adopted in recent scholarship on Romans. The heart of Romans is not found in either chapters 1–4 ("justification by faith") or chapters 5–8 ("mystical union with Christ") but in chapters 9–11: Who now constitutes the people of God? This approach is part of a larger revolution in approaches to Paul and Judaism, dubbed the "new perspective on Paul."[2]

Answers to the question of who constitutes the people of God differ. This is true for both the first and twenty-first centuries. Jews/Israel claim the title for themselves. They had it first, and by their lights, they have kept it. I am not aware of diatribes composed by Jews against the church/Christianity for assuming, by their lights, that the title has transferred to them. Perhaps it does not occur to a lot of Jews to raise the question because they are satisfied with the traditional assumption of the Jews being the chosen people of God. But Christians like Paul do ask it. Now, in the twenty-first century, so do Messianic Jews. It is a question of soteriology.

The Test of Viability

This book proceeds along the premise that in order for Messianic Judaism to be viable:

- it cannot reject Judaism as a false or failed religion of unsaved people;
- nor can it take on the rights and privileges of belonging to the church while shunning Christian orthodoxy.

Positively, it can affirm both religions as true for its members and practitioners in a way that is not for people whose truth is in Messianic Judaism. Our theological understanding is of three partners in the service of the same God who is revealed in the Bible.

This Bible study on the book of Romans looks at Paul's struggle with his dual identity as a Jew and as a Christian and how he reconciled the new gospel with the on-going reality of Judaism and its truth claims. The project originated as an assignment at the New Calvary School of Ministry in Wilmington, Delaware in 2014 in which I used two lenses to look at each verse, Christian and Messianic or, as I have labeled them here, Devotional and Critical. The critical Messianic approach reveals the trustworthiness of

---

2. Moo, *Romans*, 25.

Judaism despite Paul's muddlements. This affirmation is necessary in Messianic Jewish religion because if Judaism is shown to be unsound, Messianic Judaism would be falsified as well. All that would be left is Christianity—and we should all join that.

Introduction

The book of Romans is first in the order of the New Testament epistles. Paul's epistles were given primacy over the others, and they are ordered according to their length. Romans is the longest of Paul's letters. It is less occasioned by circumstances than his other letters to churches. To the church in the capital city he gives his greatest account of his teaching and preaching of the gospel, a word he coined for the message God laid upon him to deliver to the churches, the synagogues and the world.

Commonly, an outline of the book of Romans recognizes a break between the end of chapter 8 and the beginning of chapter 9, as well as a break between the doxology at the end of chapter 11 and the beginning of chapter 12. Chapters 9—11 are a unit in which Paul wrestles with the difficulties arising from his conviction that a separation exists between the Jewish people and salvation. The salvation, or justification, given and obtained through Christ is assumed here to be an offer that Jewish people have refused. No particular Jewish responses are given; the rejection is simply a premise. The book of Acts says that Jews from Antioch and Iconium followed Paul to Lystra and stoned him there for preaching the gospel of Jesus Christ, perhaps giving him enough experience of Jewish rejection to be confident of its reality in relationship to God.

Building upon his thrilling affirmations of the power of God unto salvation in chapter 8, Paul now expounds upon the grace of God that is manifested through our election in Christ.

Comparing Terms and Usage

Messianic Judaism as I have introduced it is an unorthodox set of beliefs in the Christian sense—as is Judaism, of course. If Judaism stands as a true religion then Christianity does not have exclusivity with God, which is Pauline orthodoxy. If instead Christianity is one among a set of authentic biblical religions then the door is opened for Messianic Judaism. The soteriology of Messianic Judaism is related to the truth in Christian-Jewish relations. The heart of the matter lies in Paul's struggle with the validity of Judaism in light of his revelation of Jesus Christ. Romans 9—11 is the passage of scripture where Paul's struggle plays out. I will show how he fails to dismiss the sacred claims of Judaism and the Jews as false.

Paul writes about Judaism and the Jews in three ways in the book of Romans. The first way is the most frequent and with the plainest sense. For example, the terms in 11:1 are clear designations: "I ask then: Did God reject *his people*? By no means! I am *an Israelite* myself, a *descendent of Abraham, from the tribe of Benjamin.*" Other occurrences of the plain sense are in the words: "my people"—10:21; "the people of Israel"—11:7; "my kinsmen"—9:3; "Israel"—10:19; "all Israel"—11:26; "Zion"—9:33; "the others"—11:7; "some of the branches"—11:17; "the natural branches"—11:21; "Jacob"—11:26.

The second way Paul writes about the same subject is in the context of a distinction between natural and spiritual identities, claiming that a minority or remnant of natural Jews are also spiritual Jews. For example, in 11:7 he writes, "What then? What the people of Israel sought so earnestly they did not obtain. *The elect* among them did, but the others were hardened." Other occurrences of the spiritual sense are in the word "remnant"—9:27; 11:5.

The third way of writing about Judaism and the Jews has a still different meaning. It has the sense of the true Israel or God's Israel. In 9:6, Paul writes, "It is not as though God's word had failed. For not all who are descended from Israel are *Israel*." The meaning of the second term is a critical observation. Its definition differs from those in the other occurrences of the same word. This use undercuts all his arguments for Jewish insufficiency. In 11:16–18, the idea of an established people of God appears again in the designations *"root of the olive tree"* and *"the root."* It is not clear that Paul even recognizes how his case against the Jews slips away with his application of these terms. Their appearance is proof that Paul could not ultimately escape the reality that Judaism is a true religion. This is the distinction that opens the door for Messianic Judaism: God's chosen people existing apart from the church and the election through Jesus Christ alone. The God of the Bible is not exclusively working with the Christians. There is more than one seat at God's table and now Messianic Jews are taking their place.

NIV Text and Dual Commentary

9:1–4a

> I speak the truth in Christ—I am not lying, my conscience confirms it through the Holy Spirit— ² I have great sorrow and unceasing anguish in my heart. ³ For I could wish that I myself

were cursed and cut off from Christ for the sake of my people, those of my own race, ⁴ the people of Israel.

Devotional

Literally, *Truth I say in Christ*. "Truth" stands out as the first word that accomplishes a break from his train of thought in chapter 8. Before establishing the truth of his message, he gives us the stamp of his personal integrity: he is speaking truly. The preceding verse at the conclusion of chapter 8 renders the full title "Christ Jesus our Lord"; the use of a title for the Savior rather than his personal name directs us to Paul's personal experience of Jesus Christ as a heavenly master and Lord revealed to him on the road to Damascus.

The chapter divisions in this section (made by Stephen Langton in 1227) may have drawn upon the repetition of the word "heart" in 9:1 and 10:1. Chapter 9 begins with "anguish in my heart"; chapter 10 begins with "the desire of my heart": a negative appeal followed by a positive appeal, both concerning the salvation of the Jews. Contrariwise, Paul begins identifying himself with the Jews "my people," (9:3), but disassociates himself by the beginning of chapter 10: "[T]hat they might be saved" (10:1). The Nestle-Aland Greek text renders verses 9:3–5 as one long run-on sentence.

Critical

The phrase "in Christ" is Pauline—a trademark of his—and becomes a vital tool in building his argument when, in 9:7, he easily adapts it to be, for the Jews, "in Isaac" (KJV). Note how Paul qualifies "truth" as "truth in Christ" and "conscience" as "conscience in the Holy Spirit." At the start he seals his argument with the Jews by defining his terms in a Christian way.

9:4–5

⁴ the people of Israel. Theirs is the adoption to sonship; theirs the divine glory, the covenants, the receiving of the law, the temple worship and the promises. ⁵ Theirs are the patriarchs, and from them is traced the human ancestry of the Messiah, who is God over all, forever praised! Amen.

Devotional

Note the progression through seven blessings building up to "the Messiah" (NIV 2011; or "the Christ" in NIV 1984). This reflects Paul's belief that the Christ is the fulfillment of all of the acts of God that have come before. The final act is superior by virtue of the sequence. Here it is implied that Christ is the most comprehensive revelation, supplanting the earlier ones.

The end of verse 5 can be translated two ways: either, as here, "... *the Messiah, who is God over all, forever praised!*" Or as, "... *the Christ. God who is over all be blessed forever*" (RSV).

The first affirms the Messiah as the incarnation of God; the second does not. "God over all" is another subject in another sentence. A word study of *eulogestos*, "praised, blessed," supports the RSV punctuation because all other occurrences of this word (Rom 1:25; 2 Cor 1:3; 2 Cor 3:11) are applied only to God the Father, not to the Christ (Messiah). This also makes good sense for Paul's argument—that God does not belong to Israel or to the church or to any of us, but is over all.

Critical

Paul introduces adoption here only to negate it in the next paragraph ("to sonship" is not in the Greek text). Something failed (9:6). It is not clear what. Then comes "Nor . . . are they all Abraham's children" (9:7). Paul leaves it to the reader to conclude that some Jews (Many? Most? All who do not confess Jesus is Lord?) have failed adoptions. Note the absence of "election" in this list of blessings. Others would certainly include that. The climax of the sequence is the Christ. He is over all of us without qualification (NIV; not RSV). But in 10:4, Paul will write "For Christ is the end (*telos*) of the law for righteousness to everyone that believeth" (KJV), qualifying the reign of Christ over us in a way that excludes nonbelievers (the Jews).

9:6

> [6] It is not as though God's word had failed. For not all who are descended from Israel are Israel.

Devotional

Paul sometimes uses Hebrew parallelism in his Greek writing (cf. 1 Cor 1:26-29), repeating an idea in different words. Here "the word of God" is parallel with "the word of promise" in 9:9. Christian thinkers distinguish between the visible church and the invisible church in like manner to Paul's distinction between "descended from Israel" and being "Israel." God judges our hearts while people can only judge by appearances.

Critical

If ever there was a case to be made for putting a word of scripture in italics for emphasis or in quotation marks for accentuation, the second occurrence of "Israel" in 9:6 is it. Paul uses the name differently here than elsewhere. He could have written "true Israel" and said the same thing. This Israel is parallel to "the children of promise . . . Abraham's offspring" in 9:8. But after 9:8, they disappear from the discourse. This party is not the "remnant chosen by grace" in 11:5. That would be Jews in the church of Christ, "those other branches" (11:18), clearly not who Paul refers to here. Some theologians make sense of this verse by thinking of the church as the true people of God, the true Israel, who inherited this mantle from the Jews. How arrogant. Does Paul just make a slip here, conceding that there is an Israel of Jews that is okay with God, like the invisible church?

9:7-9

> ⁷ Nor because they are his descendants are they all Abraham's children. On the contrary, "It is through Isaac that your offspring will be reckoned." ⁸ In other words, it is not the children by physical descent who are God's children, but it is the children of the promise who are regarded as Abraham's offspring. ⁹ For this was how the promise was stated: "At the appointed time I will return, and Sarah will have a son."

Devotional

Paul is insisting that the miracle of Sarah giving birth in her barrenness is the act of God that produced a word of promise—parallel with "word of God" in 9:6 and, perhaps, "word of faith" in 10:8. The covenant through

Isaac (Greek "*in* Isaac") is given in Gen 17:21. To the Galatians, Paul wrote earlier, "Now you, brothers and sisters, like Isaac, are children of promise" (Gal 4:28). "Children by physical descent," in contrast, refers to Abraham's other son by Hagar, Ishmael, whose birth was not miraculous. Furthermore, "If you belong to Christ, then you are Abraham's seed, and heirs according to the promise" (Gal 3:29).

Critical

Verse 9:8 could be counted as evidence that Paul is a self-loathing Jew. He redefines the common definition of Jewry to exclude all but a remnant of the Jewish population along with himself. Commonly, Jews then and now have an identity forged in the experience of the exodus from slavery in Egypt under the leadership of Moses, involving the giving of the Torah in a Sinaic covenant. In this way Jews speak of their election as a people set apart. The promises of God in the Torah are received in relation to the commandments (law) that accompany them. Both commands and promises are counted as gracious gifts.

Paul coins the Greek phrase "in Isaac" for Jews to mirror his use of "in Christ" for Christians and "in Adam" for all people (Rom 8:1; 1 Cor 15:22). When I asked Rabbi Michael Beals of the Conservative Congregation Beth Shalom about Jews being in Isaac he had no idea what I was talking about, Gen 17:21 not withstanding. Paul wants to trace the promise of God in Jesus Christ to an origin in Jewish scripture and tradition. Messianic Judaism wants to do the same but without excluding the Jews from the promise of God in the process. If Paul had seen Moses and Elijah standing alongside Jesus in heaven he might have developed a simpler soteriology in which both Jews and Christians are saved.

9:10–13

> [10] Not only that, but Rebekah's children were conceived at the same time by our father Isaac. [11] Yet, before the twins were born or had done anything good or bad—in order that God's purpose in election might stand: [12] not by works but by him who calls—she was told, "The older will serve the younger." [13] Just as it is written: "Jacob I loved, but Esau I hated."

Devotional

Here again Paul connects God's purpose with his foreknowledge of individuals who receive his calling. This was part of the order of salvation Paul offered in the previous chapter: 8:28–30. There he introduced the idea of predestination. Here he substitutes the term "election" for this certainty of God's choices in people. God is at work but not in response to any human need or merit. What comes to us has its source in God alone even as it embraces our faith and good works. This is most clearly stated by saying that our lives are captured by God, whether we are yet cognizant of it or not. We receive our lives from God, we do not invent them ourselves.

Critical

It is ironic that Paul uses a verse saying "Jacob I loved" to demonstrate that, since he rejected the Messiah, Jacob is no longer loved. The role of Esau (Edom) is assigned to the Jews (Israel), and the Christians now star as Jacob in the drama of salvation. On the contrary, the passage in Malachi is a word of the Lord to Israel in which the Lord says, "I have loved you" (Mal 1:1–2). We will see Paul use Jewish scriptures of prophetic correction to vacate the Jewish religion but here he does it with a Jewish scripture about God's judgment on one of their enemies.

9:14–16

> [14] What then shall we say? Is God unjust? Not at all! [15] For he says to Moses, "I will have mercy on whom I have mercy, and I will have compassion on whom I have compassion." [16] It does not, therefore, depend on human desire or effort, but on God's mercy.

Devotional

A transliteration of verses 14 and 16 is an improvement upon this translation. Verse 14, literally: "What therefore shall we say? Not, unrighteousness with God. May it not be." Verse 16, literally: "So therefore not of the wishing nor of the running but of the one having mercy: God."

Election and predestination demonstrate the sovereignty of God over all things. There is nothing above God's freedom, God's will, God's choices, God's acts. "God is love" is a description of a sovereign God (1 John 4:8); "Love is God" sounds similar but would put God beneath a higher idea or standard of love. Mercy is another high idea and standard that God is over, not under. Mercy answers to God, God does not answer to mercy. He is free that way. Justice answers to God, God does not answer to justice. God is above all things, so does not have to treat everyone the same (e.g., Ishmael and Esau). Paul's position is that God is not obligated by anything, even his covenants with the offspring of Abraham and Isaac.

Critical

Jews believe instead that one of God's sovereign choices was to obligate himself to Israel through his covenants. Messianic Jews go further and add the new covenant in Messiah Yeshua to that same list.

Paul has no interest here in covenantal theology, however. Instead he will purse the idea of righteousness and unrighteousness in 9:30–31 and 10:3–4; while we shall not say "unrighteousness with God," we (Paul) shall say "unrighteousness with Israel." That is a shift away from emphasizing God's sovereign role in determining salvation.

9:17–18

> [17] For Scripture says to Pharaoh: "I raised you up for this very purpose, that I might display my power in you and that my name might be proclaimed in all the earth." [18] Therefore God has mercy on whom he wants to have mercy, and he hardens whom he wants to harden.

Devotional

Verse 18 is nine words in Greek and nineteen words in this English translation. Literally it is, "So therefore whom he wishes he has mercy, but whom he wishes he hardens." The Greek verb *thelo* used in verse 16 ("of the wishing") recurs here in verse 18, but would be better translated "to will"; that is, better translated, "To whom he wills he has mercy but, on the other hand, to whom he wills he hardens." So it is not human wishing or willing that counts but God's wishing and willing. While Esau may have been bad from the womb, Pharaoh represents the sinner in a clearer way. Raising up a sinner is not a matter of God imputing more sin. It is better understood as God standing back and allowing the man's sin to have an even greater expression and rise. Paul's point is that God is an actor in both sides of the drama of Pharaoh's wickedness and defeat for a logical purpose: that God's good name might be proclaimed.

Critical

Here Paul introduces another enemy of Israel with the same result that soon the Jews will be cast in this role, opposite to the historical record and opposite to their self-understanding. Displaying "power" here is synonymous with the wrath of God. The wrath of God was upon Pharaoh in olden days; now the wrath of God is upon the Jews (9:22). This is the fourth occurrence of the Greek word *dynamis* (power) in Romans (also 1:4, 16, 20). Compare the English word "dynamite." Initially, God "declared with power" Jesus "to be the Son of God by his resurrection from the dead" (1:4) and revealed the gospel as "the power of God for the salvation of everyone who believes" (1:16). Now this "power" manifests a dark side, from the human point of view, as God's wrath.

9:19–23

> [19] One of you will say to me: "Then why does God still blame us? For who is able to resist his will?" [20] But who are you, a human being, to talk back to God? "Shall what is formed say to the one who formed it, 'Why did you make me like this?'" [21] Does not the potter have the right to make out of the same lump of clay some pottery for special purposes and some for common use? [22] What if God, although choosing to show his wrath and make his power known, bore with great patience the objects of his wrath—prepared for destruction? [23] What if he did this to make the riches of his glory known to the objects of his mercy, whom he prepared in advance for glory.

Devotional

Note the six question marks, with the final sentence leading to a seventh. The reader assists in the persuasion by answering in her own voice. Here Paul interrupts his exposition of Hebrew scripture to imagine a story of God's judgment. The translation of verse 19 was revised in the updated NIV as "Who is able to resist his will?" rather than "Who resists his will?" We do not have the capacity to resist even if we wanted to. Infralapsarianism is a theological belief in a decree of salvation for some which emanated from eternity upon God's foreknowledge of the fall of humanity into sin. It assumes the people are fixed in their respective positions as saved or damned and that no one damned can attain salvation apart from the decree that went forth without his name on it. That would be an attempt to defy God's sovereignty and foreknowledge that he established in pre-existence. Everything is fixed.

Paul does not answer his questions because silence is the appropriate response. This silence is an end to our thoughts and judgments. In turn, God is free to be silent. God is free to be the Other, outside and apart from our thoughts and questions. On the other hand, there is the answer of glory for some of us, waiting at the end for those who were prepared in advance to receive it.

Critical

The Greek text does not literally ask, "Then why does God still blame us?" Rather it asks, "Then why does God still blame?" or "Why still finds he fault?" But the NIV's insertion of "us" tips Paul's hand because the idea of the Jews getting the blame dominates Paul's thinking. To whom does "us" refer? The blame of Christians is covered but not the blame of the Jews, whose sin of rejecting the Messiah is unforgivable if they do not repent of it and join the church. Such objects of wrath serve to glorify God by their defeat. It is as though the Jews are in Isaac on Abraham's altar being sacrificed for the worship of God.

9:23–26

> [23] What if he did this to make the riches of his glory known to the objects of his mercy, whom he prepared in advance for

glory—[24] even us, whom he also called, not only from the Jews but also from the Gentiles?

[25] As he says in Hosea:

"I will call them 'my people' who are not my people; and I will call her 'my loved one' who is not my loved one,"

[26] and, "In the very place where it was said to them, 'You are not my people,' there they will be called 'children of the living God.'"

Devotional

At 1:18 Paul began the book of Romans by saying that the wrath of God "is being revealed against all the godlessness and wickedness of people." So, though "Christ died for the ungodly" (5:6), godlessness and wickedness remain—apart from the ones for whom Christ died (5:8), chosen to be "saved from God's wrath through him!" (5:9). Now addressing the saved at the church, Paul teaches that there is a revelation in the wrath of God for those looking on in security. Concealed in the ongoing judgment and anger of God are "the riches of his glory." Paul finds parallels to "even us" (9:24) in the renaming of the saved in the time of Hosea.

Critical

What an unfortunate misreading of one of the early literary prophets. Here Paul chooses to quote the only Jew of the northern kingdom whose writings were canonized, a prophet who addressed that society. They are known to history as the lost tribes of Israel because in their exile they assimilated with their captors and gave up their identity as "children of the living God." These facts are ignored here. So how great is the irony! The very ones who were not saved are brought on stage as forerunners of the saved through God's mercy, God's election, God's foreknowledge. This did not happen.

Paul would have done better to remind us instead of the Ninevites to whom Jonah preached. But there is no remnant in that story and his argument requires one. Yet there was no remnant from the northern kingdom either. He is drawn to Hosea for the phrase "You are not my people" which Paul reimagines as being addressed to the nations, the *ethnos*, the Gentiles. Gentiles were also estranged from God, like the Jews of the northern kingdom. The name "You are not my people" fits them too. Paul is applying his

9:27–30

> [27] Isaiah cries out concerning Israel:
> "Though the number of the Israelites be like the sand by the sea, only the remnant will be saved. [28] For the Lord will carry out his sentence on earth with speed and finality."
> [29] It is just as Isaiah said previously:
> "Unless the Lord Almighty had left us descendants, we would have become like Sodom, we would have been like Gomorrah."
> [30] What then shall we say? That the Gentiles, who did not pursue righteousness, have obtained it, a righteousness that is by faith;

Devotional

Isaiah was a prophet to the southern kingdom (Judah), addressed here as Israel. His prediction of the survival of a remnant was prescient. It is a striking example of the mercy of God at work in the world. Verse 9:30a is the turning point, the summing up, of Paul's argument. Compare 8:31a. What then shall we say? We shall say two things, for the salvation paradigm is two-sided. First, God's promise and God's mercy brings with it the gift of faith. Compare 9:8 and 9:16. Secondly, Paul emphasizes the other side of the experience, the grasp of faith that obtains the prize.

Critical

How does Paul arrive at justification by faith? He reintroduces the faith of Abraham in God's promise after applying his either/or paradigm by way of Bible verses on God's election. Why didn't he shorten his argument by taking us directly from the faith of Abraham (9:8–9) to the faith of the Gentiles (9:30)? Instead he breaks it up with, "Not only that, but. . ." in 9:10. By this addition (twenty verses), he establishes that God is on the side of the believers in Christ. The believing Gentiles and Jewish remnant are not only justified by their faith, they are justified by a decision of God. So if you oppose Paul's arguments, you not only oppose Paul, you oppose God.

The church of Jesus Christ is God's church, God's previous election of Israel notwithstanding.

The battleground has shifted from covenantal faithfulness to justification by faith. Neither the Torah of Moses nor the prophecies of Hosea or Isaiah conceived of an individual being made righteous or just in the sense of Paul's gospel. Judaism is a communal faith practiced in families. But Paul was alone in his conversion experience—his companions did not hear the voice. A nation or a tribe or a family can not take up a cross and follow Jesus because there is no collective cross, no collective dying, no collective baptism, no collective rising. The promise of God in Romans is for individuals to realize. Messianic Judaism is a third way, embracing both the communal nature of Judaism and the personal calling of Christianity.

9:31-33

> [31] but the people of Israel, who pursued the law as the way of righteousness, have not attained their goal. [32] Why not? Because they pursued it not by faith but as if it were by works. They stumbled over the stumbling stone. [33] As it is written:
> "See, I lay in Zion a stone that causes people to stumble and a rock that makes them fall, and the one who believes in him will never be put to shame."

Devotional

How we pursue the goal of being justified, of being righteous, makes all the difference to our success or failure. In every path there will be a stone to deal with, called a stumbling stone by those who fail and called a cornerstone by those who succeed. Unrighteous people logically take offense at the judgment and wrath of a righteous God against sin. Overcoming this offense by faith is the great possibility of being human. Other ways of trying to get around that stone always fail.

Critical

Paul concludes his argument against the soundness of the Jewish faith with quotations from Isaiah 8:14b and 28:16. But he takes these verses out of context. Messianic Judaism insists that Hebrew scriptures be read both in their own context and in the light of the revelation of Messiah Yeshua. Of course, Jews do not study this way. Do Christians? Often Christians follow the practice, pioneered by Paul, of using Old Testament verses for a purpose other than the one their author intended. In Isaiah 28:14–22, the prophet is delivering news that the wrath of God has come, that the Lord Almighty has decreed destruction against the whole land (28:22). Meanwhile, leaders are boasting of their untouchability when "an overwhelming scourge" (Assyria) sweeps by (28:15). In the midst of God's wrath is God's mercy: "I lay a stone in Zion, a tested stone, a precious cornerstone for a sure foundation; the one who trusts will never be dismayed" (28:16). What a tremendous challenge for a human being: to trust in God in the midst of war, in the midst of an alien invasion that God will not stop. This trust in God, a personal leap of faith in the face of overwhelming evidence to the contrary, would compare favorably with any act of faith.

Paul is not interested. It does not fit into his agenda of mining the Hebrew Bible for verses that can be understood either as predictions of the messiahship of Jesus or as evidence of God's rejection of traditional Judaism which Christianity has supplanted. The gospel trumps the Hebrew scriptures. No prior revelation of God and no prior faith in God has legitimacy apart from God's revelation in Jesus Christ. The old always gives way to the new. Messianic Jews disagree with this premise and proceed to honor the God of Judaism and God in Christ as one God who revealed himself both in the Torah and in Yeshua's appearing without contradiction. It gets us to the goal (9:31).

10:1–2

> ¹ Brothers and sisters, my heart's desire and prayer to God for the Israelites is that they may be saved. ² For I can testify about them that they are zealous for God, but their zeal is not based on knowledge.

Devotional

"[T]hey ... about them ... but their ..." are pronouns in 10:1–2 that contrast in perspective with the same writer's statement, "I am an Israelite" in 11:1. The writer is someone else at the start of chapter 10, but is present company at the start of chapter 11. The church Paul helped lead as an apostle can be remembered as one party in the fractured Jewish society of first-century

Israel. Verses 1:7 and 10:1 are evidence that, from the start, being a Christian meant being set apart from the other Jewish traditions. That is how they understood themselves.

Critical

Verse 10:1 could easily be an English translation of a Hebrew sentence written by Isaiah or Jeremiah. However their understanding of being saved differed markedly from Paul's. Without the revelation of the gospel, Isaiah or Jeremiah could not conceive of salvation from sin on Paul's terms. To a Jew, "being saved" would be an experience of God's deliverance from particular and concrete threats, through which God's love and sovereignty are affirmed. That is not a part of Paul's prayer (10:1). The knowledge they lack is of the gospel, not of God and his ways.

10:3–4

> [3] Since they did not know the righteousness of God and sought to establish their own, they did not submit to God's righteousness. [4] Christ is the culmination of the law so that there may be righteousness for everyone who believes.

Devotional

In our experience, the righteousness of God is a gift. Conceiving of it on any other terms turns it into something else. Paul's idea is that the opposite of a gift is a labor or work. When the gift takes the form of the atoning sacrifice of Jesus on the cross (3:25), turning it into something else is an offense to the giver and to all who loved Jesus's appearing. Paul separates himself from the unknowledgeable. The prize that Israelites seek so zealously is offered by Christ, but only on his terms.

Critical

Paul appears to consider Judaism to be a failed experiment. God has moved on. The coming of Christ is another attempt by God to do what he failed to accomplish in his first initiative through the Jews. Paul does not take seriously the covenantal promises of God to Israel. His notion of unconditional grace is defined by contrast to the law, against the Torah. How could he miss so much of the truth of the Torah being a gift? Perhaps the experience of conversion led him to reject his past and the grace of God in it.

10:5–7

> [5] Moses writes this about the righteousness that is by the law: "The person who does these things will live by them." [6] But the righteousness that is by faith says: "Do not say in your heart, 'Who will ascend into heaven?'" (that is, to bring Christ down) [7] "or 'Who will descend into the deep?'" (that is, to bring Christ up from the dead).

Devotional

Verse 10:5 is a close parallel to Jesus's teaching in the Sermon on the Mount. Compare Matthew 7:24–27, in which the only difference between the wise man and the fool is in the doing by one and the not doing by the other. Verse 10:5b is literally, "The doing man will live by it." Verse 10:6 follows with "But the of-faith righteousness thus says."

Then the confusion begins for many readers. Verses 6b and 7 are either a bridge or a gap between verses 10:6a and 8, depending on what a person can make of them. They could be omitted and would never be missed. They provide a contrast to "in your mouth and in your heart" (10:8) and "believe in your heart" (10:9). It is possible to miss Christ if your heart looks outward instead of inward in the moment of faith and trust.

Critical

The more obvious contrast is between "the righteousness that is by the law" and "the righteousness that is by faith." In the first case, the person of deeds lives by them. In the second case (10:9), the person of faith ends up simply declaring and believing in his heart. Certainly this is a false choice. The person of deeds also declares and believes in her heart. The person of faith also lives by his imputed righteousness. What else could he do? He has got to live. Messianic Judaism rejects this false choice and embraces God's imputed righteousness as both according to the deeds of the law (Torah) and according to faith.

10:8–10

> ⁸ But what does it say? "The word is near you; it is in your mouth and in your heart," that is, the message concerning faith that we proclaim: ⁹ If you declare with your mouth, "Jesus is Lord," and believe in your heart that God raised him from the dead, you will be saved. ¹⁰ For it is with your heart that you believe and are justified, and it is with your mouth that you profess your faith and are saved.

Devotional

Paul's first mention of *kerysso* ("to proclaim, to preach") was in 2:21, speaking of the Jews preaching their admonitions. Now Paul has in mind a very particular, exclusively Christian kind of preaching concerning the "word of faith" (KJV; NIV 1984)—rendered above as "the message concerning faith." The communication event that is Christian preaching calls for a response from the listener, as these verses explain. But the message itself is in response to a pre-existing condition or question. Here Paul says it is the absence of righteousness or justification. Preachers are sent forth "so that there may be righteousness" (10:4). Note the parallelism in 10:10, matching being justified with being saved.

Critical

In the center of Paul's explanation of preaching is the conjunction "if," implicitly joining two propositions: "If . . . then . . ." There is no "if" in Judaism because every Jew is born a Jew, born into the covenant relationship. One may become a lazy Jew, a corrupted Jew, an unfaithful Jew, or a bad Jew, but the Jewish identity is never conditional. Then came the apostle Paul and Christian preaching and conversions. The Messianic Jewish minority makes an unPauline distinction between Jews and Gentiles—between Jews and everyone else. We recognize the Jewish birthright of a covenantal relationship. The new covenant in Messiah Yeshua does not negate this; it can only add to it. It is a mistake to preach to a Jewish audience the same way one preaches to a secular audience of unbelievers. There are different assumptions. Some people are born justified (chosen). That is both a blessing and a burden.

10:11–13

> [11] As Scripture says, "Anyone who believes in him will never be put to shame." [12] For there is no difference between Jew and Gentile—the same Lord is Lord of all and richly blesses all who call on him, [13] for, "Everyone who calls on the name of the Lord will be saved."

Devotional

Paul has introduced specific content into what a justified person believes since he last quoted Isaiah 28:16 in verse 9:33. It is nothing less than a miracle. The faith that saves is a faith that can affirm that the man Jesus who died is now alive, having been raised from death by the power of God (10:9). There is no worldly basis for such an affirmation, no logical rationale rooted in facts, for facts are established by the scientific method. The absence of righteousness (justification) can only be remedied from above by a gift or a grasp of transcendence. Apart from a miracle, we remain stuck in imminence. A preacher would say we remain lost in it. The possibility of being found by the Lord—of being saved—is only a hope until that possibility is realized by faith.

Critical

Here is another unfortunate misreading of a prophetic word in the Old Testament. Joel 2:32, quoted in 10:13, should properly read: "Everyone *of you* who calls on the name of the Lord will be saved."

Chapter 2 of the book of Joel contains three oracles from the Lord, set off by quotation marks in the New International Version. Verse 2:32 is in the center of the third oracle, which begins at 2:25 and ends at 3:8, followed by the words, "The Lord has spoken." The Lord speaks from "I" to "you." The twelve appearances of "you" and "your" in the part of the oracle preceding 2:32 establish the Jewish context of this verse Paul was drawn to. The Lord means to say "Every one *of you Jews* who calls on the name of the Lord will be saved," but it got truncated in its translation into Greek in Romans 10:13.

Of course the Lord has a definite word on what he will save them from: an apocalypse. It is not from sin or unrighteousness or unbelief as Paul mistakenly supposes. Was this mistake creative license? Is Paul guilty of a deliberate misapplication of Joel's prophecy? It may be unfair to judge

Paul by contemporary standards of Bible study. A verse's original setting is not a boundary to Paul. But today, any college freshman in Religion 101 would have to do better.

10:14–16

> [14] How, then, can they call on the one they have not believed in? And how can they believe in the one of whom they have not heard? And how can they hear without someone preaching to them? [15] And how can anyone preach unless they are sent? As it is written: "How beautiful are the feet of those who bring good news!"
> [16] But not all the Israelites accepted the good news. For Isaiah says, "Lord, who has believed our message?"

Devotional

A string of four questions building upon one another is a rhetorical flourish. The climactic appeal for more preachers leaves the reader hanging in suspense. How can it possibly happen? Then we learn that help is coming. God has heard our cries. The good news—literally "good good news" or "glad tidings of good things!" (10:15 KJV)—is being sent. It is being sent from above, which gives it power to save. Verse 10:16 would be better translated "But not all the Israelites harkened to the gospel." The King James Version is "But they have not all obeyed the gospel." This is a new idea. Israelites obey the law, obey the teachings, obey the commandments, and obey the Torah. Paul is the first to say that they should also obey the gospel.

Critical

The Orthodox Jewish Bible (OJB) helpfully translates the start of 10:14 in a literal fashion, "How therefore shall they call on him in whom they have not believed?" The subordinating conjunction "therefore" points both backwards and forwards: back to the quotation of Joel 2:32 and forward to "the one they have not believed in." How did the messiahship of Jesus and his resurrection from the dead become the standard for belief in God? By Paul's gospel. Not by anything in Judaism. In one stroke the Jews have gone from being the people of God to being atheists. One day they were in covenant with God; the next day Paul was confronted by Jesus from heaven and they were men and women of unbelief. Jews do not think so of themselves. Messianic Jews should not think so either.

In most Bibles, the name for God in Joel 2:32 is written as "the LORD" in place of the Tetragrammaton. In his quotation of the verse (10:13), Paul adapts it to "the Lord." If you are only hearing Paul's letter read you would not catch the change. But Joel's Hebrew verse is about calling on God. Paul's Greek quotation of it is about calling on Jesus. The first Greek translation of Joel, the Septuagint, substitutes *kyrios* (Lord) for the name of God. That is also how Paul refers to Jesus. Even if Jesus is Lord we cannot project him back into every verse of the Old Testament in which the Septuagint uses the word *kyrios* for God's name, including Adonai as well. But that is the sense of the appeal in Romans 10:14b, "And how can they believe in the one whom they have not heard?" which follows upon the Joel quotation. Of course the Jews have heard of the LORD. But they have not heard of the Lord Jesus. "Therefore" is there to drag them into Paul's appeals and to switch Joel 2:32 into a prophecy about Jesus Christ.

10:17–18

> [17] Consequently, faith comes from hearing the message, and the message is heard through the word about Christ. [18] But I ask: Did they not hear? Of course they did: "Their voice has gone out into all the earth, their words to the ends of the world."

Devotional

Preaching gives voice to "the gospel of God" (1:1) or "my gospel" (2:16); also named "the word (*logos*) of God" (9:6), "the word (*rhema*) of faith" (10:8) or "good things" (*agatha*, 10:15). There is a disagreement among the Greek manuscripts regarding how Paul ends 10:17. The manuscripts used by the earliest translators (the Geneva Bible in 1599; the King James Version in 1611; the Darby Bible in 1867) said "word (*rhema*) of God." Many of us learned it as, "So then faith cometh by hearing, and hearing *by the word of God*" (KJV). All modern English translations, the NIV included, rely on earlier Greek manuscripts and say "the word of Christ." The NIV muddles the translation by twice adding "the message" to aid the reader. There is no corresponding word for it in the Greek text.

Critical

The idea that hearing comes by the word of Christ leads into Paul's saying in 11:25, "Israel has experienced a hardening in part." The idea is that humanity never really heard from God until Paul (or Jesus?) began to preach. Some Christians today believe this; others do not. Messianic Jews must not. I suppose if the book of Psalms is attached to your pocket New Testament you recognize that some Jews heard from God before the coming of Jesus.

10:19–21

> [19] Again I ask: Did Israel not understand? First, Moses says,
> "I will make you envious by those who are not a nation; I will make you angry by a nation that has no understanding."
> [20] And Isaiah boldly says,
> "I was found by those who did not seek me; I revealed myself to those who did not ask for me."
> [21] But concerning Israel he says,
> "All day long I have held out my hands to a disobedient and obstinate people."

Devotional

God is making his appeal. Compare 2 Corinthians 5:20. God is a lover, actively seeking his beloved. Compare Hosea 2:14–23. The initiative for a covenant lies in God. The gift of faith always precedes the grasp of it. Jews, Christians, and Messianic Jews can agree that Isaiah's picture of God facing us with his hands held out all day long is a true one that shows a love from beyond that is more than we deserve.

Critical

Here is another unfortunate misreading of a prophetic word in the Old Testament. Isaiah 65:1, "I was found by those who did not seek me; I revealed myself to those who did not ask for me," is not a story from the nations, from the Gentiles. It is about the Jews. God (speaking through the prophet) revealed himself to Israel and was found by Israel. So the connective *de* (in English: "But" or "On the other hand") at the start of 10:21 has the effect of a ruse. It tricks the reader into thinking that the previous verse, a quotation from Isaiah 65:1, is, on the one hand, about another people beloved of God; like those to whom Moses refers in Deuteronomy 32:21, Paul's first quotation in this sequence. But Isaiah 65:1(10:20) and Isaiah 65:2 (10:21) are sentences from the same oracle, talking about the same Jews. Holding out his hands all day long is a Hebrew parallel to the saying "I revealed myself."

11:1–4

> [1] I ask then: Did God reject his people? By no means! I am an Israelite myself, a descendant of Abraham, from the tribe of Benjamin. [2] God did not reject his people, whom he foreknew. Don't you know what Scripture says in the passage about Elijah—how he appealed to God against Israel: [3] "Lord, they have killed your prophets and torn down your altars; I am the only one left, and they are trying to kill me"? [4] And what was God's answer to him? "I have reserved for myself seven thousand who have not bowed the knee to Baal."

Devotional

Paul makes his argument in a clever way. He asks three negative questions to lead to a conclusion expressed as a double negative. 1. Did they not hear?—Of course! (10:18). 2. Did Israel not understand?—They did (10:19). 3. So then, did God reject them? Noooo! (11:1). Compare 8:33: "Who will bring any charge against those whom God has chosen?" Here Israel's election manifests itself in a faithful remnant. What the prophet's ministry could not accomplish God could. Along with their election these Israelites had free will. On the one hand, being elected did not prevent them from rejecting God and freely walking away; on the other hand, having free will did not in the end undercut God's election and foreknowledge.

Critical

Just a chapter ago, at 10:1, the Jews were those other people. Here at 11:1, "I am one myself. We are all on the same side with God." He means, of course, "I am a Christian Jew" (Messianic Jew).

Can he avoid having to choose between Jesus and Moses? After all, "God did not reject his people" (11:2). Does God embrace the ways of both Jesus and Moses? Messianic Jews answer "Yes," in the sense that the righteousness of Christ fulfills the demands of the law; and "Yes," in the sense that he foreknew a remnant, as in the days of King Ahab and Elijah. But Paul is going to say that God's revelation in Moses was a covenant of works. He writes in Galatians 3:21–26 and Romans 3:19–22 that it was a warm-up act for the coming of Christ and the church. It is time to convert (11:25–26) and join the church. Do not call it rejection; think of it as a new beginning (3:28–30). Traditional Jews would think of it as assimilation and the end of Judaism.

11:5–6

> [5] So too, at the present time there is a remnant chosen by grace.
> [6] And if by grace, then it cannot be based on works; if it were, grace would no longer be grace.

Devotional

Give Paul an "A" for audacity. He truly considers the time he lives in ("the present time") as special, different from everything that has come before. God has broken into this time and is acting now as he did in the days of Elijah, as he did in the days of Moses. Paul knows something other people do not know as to what time it is: it is a time of crisis. Being a part of the minority (remnant) is sensible when riding a wave of change that will turn this minority into a new majority. Compare Romans 8:18–23; 13:11–12.

Critical

Many promises of God given in scripture are conditional (Matt 6:14; Heb 12:14; Jas 4:6; 1 John 1:7). If a person fulfills the condition, then God is able to give a gift of blessing. Note Romans 2:6b; 6:8; 8:14, 28; 15:13:

- God "will give to each person according to what he has done."
- "Now if we died with Christ, we believe that we will also live with him."
- "[B]ecause those who are led by the Spirit of God are sons of God."
- "And we know that in all things God works for the good of those who love him, who have been called according to his purpose."

- "May the God of hope fill you with all joy and peace as you trust in him, so that you may overflow with hope by the power of the Holy Spirit."

The grace/works dichotomy is a false choice. Sometimes grace is unmerited but other times it is a love or favor that fits a life, fits a choice, fits a condition. A person who is Torah observant is qualified by that for blessings that another person cannot appreciate or put to use. Such suitable blessings are God's conditional grace. Paul might characterize them as works righteousness and apply them to a scheme of salvation in such a way that they fall short of saving grace. Paul gets that way sometimes. Messianic Jews see no conflict between grace and grace: grace in the gift of Torah and grace in the gift of the sacrificial death of Yeshua.

11:7–10

[7] What then? What the people of Israel sought so earnestly they did not obtain. The elect among them did, but the others were hardened, [8] as it is written:

"God gave them a spirit of stupor, eyes that could not see and ears that could not hear, to this very day."

[9] And David says:

"May their table become a snare and a trap, a stumbling block and a retribution for them.

[10] May their eyes be darkened so they cannot see, and their backs be bent forever."

Devotional

We commonly understand our own actions to be our sovereign choices. The Bible says the same of God's actions. Here and in the alternating parts of chapter 9 (1–9; 10–29; 30–34) Paul describes two agents (divine and human) correlating their separate acts into one. Both Israel and God participated in the earnest but futile seeking of Israel. It was a real choice and action of Israel's, but it was made in the shadow of God's restraining hand. Compare God hardening the heart of Pharaoh (Exod 4:21) and consider that one act can involve divine agency, satanic agency, and human agency.

Commentary on Romans 9, 10, and 11

Critical

The quotation in verse 11:8 revises Deuteronomy 29:4 in light of the previous observation (verse 7) that "the others were hardened." Previously, Paul stated that God "hardens whom he wants to harden" (9:18). But that is not precisely how Moses spoke in Deuteronomy 29.

Originally, the Israelites have natural sight and hearing but lack the spiritual gifts from God (those "The LORD has not given") to be able to comprehend his purpose at work in their lives. But here in Romans 11:8, God curses healthy senses with a spirit of stupor to prevent them from seeing and hearing God at work as they normally could. In the former case God keeps back something; in the latter case God is striking them. In the original context of a speech by Moses in a covenant renewal ceremony it is prelude to a blessing. Moses then reveals the wonder that God held back from their understanding.

In the hands of Paul, it is God hardening their hearts so that they fail when Jesus the Messiah appears. That cuts them out of the plan and purpose of God, which is carried on instead through the elect remnant. The Messianic Jewish minority denies that God ever made that kind of move.

11:11–12

> [11] Again I ask: Did they stumble so as to fall beyond recovery? Not at all! Rather, because of their transgression, salvation has come to the Gentiles to make Israel envious. [12] But if their transgression means riches for the world, and their loss means riches for the Gentiles, how much greater riches will their full inclusion bring!

Devotional

The discourse is winding down. This is the final rhetorical question used to launch an assertion. At 9:14, 9:30, 10:19, 11:1, and here at 11:11 Paul addresses his reader yet again, "I ask now, what about this?" after quoting a verse from the Old Testament. These questions propel the argument. Paul is like a prize fighter in the boxing ring leading with jabs, pushing his way forward. Verse 11:11 is the final try. Next he will switch his approach and make an appeal directly to Gentiles, letting the Jews overhear. Then at 11:25 he turns back to his original effort and arrives at his conclusion, his knockout punch. Finally, he will say, it all comes together in the last days, at the eschaton, in the end. All Israel will be saved, their transgression not withstanding.

Critical

Paul's instruction to the church in Rome is made on a dual basis. On the one hand, it is true by the authority of his apostleship. On the other hand, it comes from the pages of the Hebrew Bible (note his opening in 1:1–2). Both are revelation. Here in 11:11–12 is an original idea that came to him as an apostle. There is no other basis for it. Some of us Messianic Jews wonder if Paul misheard God and got this one wrong. Because envy seems to be missing from the Jews' response to the coming of Christianity. For one thing a Jew would not value this salvation that Paul and Christians are so boastful of. It is alien to their self-identification as God's chosen people.

The same thing goes for the idea that just by being Jewish and holding on to their covenants they are transgressing. That Jews would envy the Christians for not being Jews because we all know Jews are bad people is an odd piece of apostolic revelation. The grand prize—"full inclusion"—is to stop being Jewish! How about instead making an appeal for Jews to retain their Judaism and still love Yeshua? It is an idea whose time has come.

11:13–16

> [13] I am talking to you Gentiles. Inasmuch as I am the apostle to the Gentiles, I take pride in my ministry [14] in the hope that I may somehow arouse my own people to envy and save some of them. [15] For if their rejection brought reconciliation to the world, what will their acceptance be but life from the dead? [16] If the part of the dough offered as firstfruits is holy, then the whole batch is holy; if the root is holy, so are the branches.

Devotional

Paul returns to God's perspective. A few verses ago (11:11–12) he described the Jews' dilemma from a human perspective: they stumbled, they committed transgressions. Even in verse 14 he has in mind Jews with free will controlling their destiny. But in verse 15 it is God who rejects and God who accepts. If God is in control—and if you are doomed—why should you be held accountable? But at the same time as he expounded election, predestination, and foreknowledge Paul also labored tirelessly to get a decision for Christ from somebody new. So he held the two sides together. The difficulty for the reader, if not for Paul, is that God is at the same time rejecting some Jews and accepting other Jews; correspondingly, some Jews are casting stones at Paul and other Jews are joining him. What to make of the Jews? The idea of an elect remnant seems to cover all cases except it still leaves a doomed population of Jews going about their Judaism, which is no longer God's plan and therefore an effrontery to God's sovereignty. In 11:15–16 he begins to speak of all Israel being saved. It stands to reason, he writes, that if a remnant is holy, then the whole batch from which it came will be holy as well. The problem disappears.

Critical

Herein (v. 15) lies the root of an evil idea that circulates in both Christian and Messianic circles today. It is that God has rejected the Jews. While the origin may lie in the writings of Paul, it was the destruction of the Temple in 70 AD, within a generation of the Jews' rejection of Jesus as their messiah, that gave this libel a life of its own. Every negative word from a Hebrew prophet was added to the weight of the accusation. The church built itself up on the bones of the Jews of Jerusalem that the Romans massacred, separating itself from the fate of that desolate city and nation in the process of telling a story about God's wrathful judgment upon people who did not love Jesus. Over the years even some depressed Jews believed it. The truth is God could no more have cut off the Jews than he could have cut off Jesus, his only begotten son. Just as Jesus suffered redemptively, so have the Jews. God's love for them will never let go. They did not have to love Jesus to stay in God's favor. A little muscle against the Romans in 70 AD would have been nice too, but God's love and favor do not always bring prosperity.

11:17–24

> [17] If some of the branches have been broken off, and you, though a wild olive shoot, have been grafted in among the others and now share in the nourishing sap from the olive root, [18] do not consider yourself to be superior to those other branches. If you do, consider this: You do not support the root, but the root supports you. [19] You will say then, "Branches were broken off so

that I could be grafted in." ²⁰ Granted. But they were broken off because of unbelief, and you stand by faith. Do not be arrogant, but tremble. ²¹ For if God did not spare the natural branches, he will not spare you either. ²² Consider therefore the kindness and sternness of God: sternness to those who fell, but kindness to you, provided that you continue in his kindness. Otherwise, you also will be cut off. ²³ And if they do not persist in unbelief, they will be grafted in, for God is able to graft them in again. ²⁴ After all, if you were cut out of an olive tree that is wild by nature, and contrary to nature were grafted into a cultivated olive tree, how much more readily will these, the natural branches, be grafted into their own olive tree!

Devotional

How to make a new start? How to begin again? Paul knows from his own experience how to do it by the power of God. See Acts 9:18: "Immediately, something like scales fell from Saul's eyes, and he could see again. He got up and was baptized." He experienced himself being broken off from the nation of Israel and grafted into the church. In his ministry to Gentiles he urges the same conversion experience from whatever a person is attached to before meeting Christ. God is both kind and stern and, more than that, God is able—able to renew Gentiles in relationship to him and the church, and if them, how much more readily the Jews as well! You want to be a part of the elect, and because that only happens by grace through faith, you should be humble and tremble.

Critical

In these six verses we have branches, shoots, roots, and trees. The olive root (vv. 16–18) is primary and foundational. The natural broken branches that God did not spare represent the Jews. But so does the olive root! The storyteller has to assume a holy Israel in order to begin the parable. This is the true Israel referenced in 9:6. Douglas Moo says the root metaphor "almost certainly represents the patriarchs," which is another way of interpreting Paul's reliance upon a genuine chosen people.[3]

The other engaging premise, of course, is the brokenness of the branches of David. When exactly was Israel broken off? When Moses found

---

3. Moo, *Romans*, 366.

the golden calf? Was that the end to God's hold on the Jews? Or was it the day they crucified our Lord, when the sky turned dark for three hours? The sun has never shined upon Israel since, metaphorically speaking—is that it? Here is another apostolic revelation: that rejecting Jesus was the unforgivable sin. Unlike any other. Unlike King David's sins this one cannot/will not/must not be forgiven or else the foundation of the church—its exclusive relationship to God and heaven and grace through the Christ event—would be undermined. If God forgives a sin apart from the atoning sacrifice on the cross the need for conversion is debatable. That just would not work. So a person who rejects Jesus does not go to heaven, does not receive God's grace, does not get through to God in prayer—he or she is broken off.

Picture a dead branch over to the side of the tree. Accepting the premise of the Jews being broken off leads to the inevitable conclusion of Jews either dying off in the course of time or converting into the church and disappearing by assimilation.

11:25–27

> [25] I do not want you to be ignorant of this mystery, brothers and sisters, so that you may not be conceited: Israel has experienced a hardening in part until the full number of the Gentiles has come in, [26] and in this way all Israel will be saved. As it is written: "The deliverer will come from Zion; he will turn godlessness away from Jacob. [27] And this is my covenant with them when I take away their sins."

Devotional

This passage begins with a pastoral concern for the wellbeing of his readers in the church in Rome. They ought not think too highly of themselves when they consider the state of the Jews in comparison with their own good fortune. They are coming into salvation, and the Jews are not. Yet. What the proud Gentile convert is ignorant about is the invisible hand of God restraining the Jews from entering in. Paul states it passively: "Israel has experienced a hardening." But it is not going to last forever. It is a stratagem. The Jews do not know it now, but soon all Israel will be saved. God would not have it any other way.

Critical

First Thessalonians is the earliest letter of Paul's preserved for the New Testament, and Romans is one of the last. They are six or seven years apart. In 1 Thessalonians 4:15, Paul writes that being alive in these final days will not be an advantage when the end comes: "According to the Lord's own word, we tell you that we who are still alive, who are left till the coming of the Lord, will certainly not precede those who have fallen asleep." In Romans 13:10–12, one sign of being in the end times is the fulfilling of the law. Another sign is the fulfillment of the Gentiles' salvation (11:25). This sense of observing around you the unfolding of humanity's ultimate destiny is behind the expression, "And in this way all Israel will be saved" (11:26).

We are standing at the finish line, so the assimilation of Israel into the church—being saved—is not a lamentable loss of Jewish culture because everything everywhere is coming to an end. There is no future in a chronological or historical sense. The Jews are not being saved unto earthly life; they are being saved unto eternal life instead—into the Christians' heaven. Paul never imagined two or three thousand years of life in the world ahead—with Jews or without Jews. So his argument comes to a close with the abrupt end to everything. There is no Jewish legacy to carry on. There is only the Christ whom Paul saw in heaven, bringing an end to every life on earth in some like manner to the way he brought an end to Saul's on the road to Damascus.

11:28–29

> [28] As far as the gospel is concerned, they are enemies for your sake; but as far as election is concerned, they are loved on account of the patriarchs, [29] for God's gifts and his call are irrevocable.

Devotional

Here Paul contrasts his two great discoveries about salvation: the gospel and election. Gospel preaching shines from the human side; election shines from the divine light. Properly understood they are interdependent. A second contrast between the enemy and the beloved manifests itself in Jewish traditions being both alien to the New Testament (enemy) and compatible (part of the Bible). By either the light of the gospel or the light of election we can be sure that the future lies in God's hand. You may doubt yourself, your choices, your abilities, your chances; but you cannot doubt your calling from God.

Critical

Israel's election is irrevocable yet the Jews are still enemies. That is Christianity. By itself this passage is proof that Christianity and Messianic Judaism are not one faith for one body of believers. The thesis of this chapter is that in regards to the gospel the Jews are that olive root from which trees and branches draw their life. The Jews are the forerunners of the gospel, the keepers of every covenant God ever made on earth and therefore also eligible for this latest new gospel covenant. Their election prior to the gospel is not "on the other hand," as Paul insists here. In the Messianic Jewish minority, we discern an inclusive vision for the same gospel and earlier election traditions.

11:30–32

> [30] Just as you who were at one time disobedient to God have now received mercy as a result of their disobedience, [31] so they too have now become disobedient in order that they too may now receive mercy as a result of God's mercy to you. [32] For God has bound everyone over to disobedience so that he may have mercy on them all.

Devotional

In conclusion Paul ties his argument back to the typology of two brothers (us and them) in chapter 9, basically restating verses 9:15–16. Note how in this conclusion Paul replaces the specifically Christian words of "saved" and "salvation" and "grace" with the more inclusive and Hebraic words of "mercy" and "receiving mercy." Here the sovereignty of God is affirmed at still higher heights. Paul's assertion that "All have sinned and fallen short" (3:23) is restated and reformulated as an act of God. Sin did not enter the world (5:12); instead God "bound everyone"—"consigned all" (RSV), "imprisoned all" (NRSV)—to disobedience. God did not just harden Pharaoh's heart. He hardened yours and mine as well. But the end justifies the means.

Our hope is that by going through disobedience and sin we may reach mercy and grace.

Critical

Paul once again libels the Jews in order to glorify God. How different from Isaiah and Jeremiah who preached that disobedience to God and his ways were failures to be corrected. Paul revels in it instead because the only way he conceives of God's mercy is as a response. Jews, on the other hand, recognize the prevenient grace in the giving of covenants that promised and delivered God's faithfulness and mercy from the start. God's mercy was theirs all the time, as his chosen people. It did not arise in God when he looked down upon their sin and disobedience, to be given in response to what just happened or in a final reckoning of a life. The rabbis know that the Jews were never without hope, never imprisoned or consigned or bound in a state of being apart from God. Nothing can take them from God's hand. They know that in their bones. The good news of Messianic Judaism is that God's faithfulness and mercy have overflowed to them in the new covenant of Yeshua the messiah, offered for adoption along with the rest of God's covenants. That is different from the Talmudic Judaism of the rabbis. It is different from Christianity. But it is not different from the Bible or from the love and purpose and plan of God.

11:33–36

> [33] Oh, the depth of the riches of the wisdom and knowledge of God! How unsearchable his judgments, and his paths beyond tracing out!
> [34] "Who has known the mind of the Lord? Or who has been his counselor?"
> [35] "Who has ever given to God, that God should repay them?"
> [36] For from him and through him and for him are all things. To him be the glory forever! Amen.

Devotional

We do well to begin an appraisal of this doxology by noting that it is followed by the words "I beseech you therefore, brethren" (12:1 KJV) that lead into five more chapters of scripture! What is the "therefore" there for? To connect this stanza of praise and wonder to everyday living. Paul's worship here is not only edifying, it is visionary: forward-looking. To enter into this doxology is to basically give up one's own quest for knowledge and answers. It is an unconditional surrender. Then we get up and move on. The day awaits us. But we are not the same as we were before we met Paul and thought his thoughts along with him. We are strengthened with new concepts, new understandings, new hopes, new determinations. He lays them all on the altar of sacrifice in 11:33–36 and gives them up. But God won't leave him alone. He is compelled to take up his pen and write still more. Paul demonstrates in his act of composition the truth of what he is writing about: mercy, election and calling.

Who is Paul addressing in this passage? The reader. He is asking rhetorical questions to which he expects no answers because now answers are beside the point. He is shutting our mouths before the glory and majesty of God. When you are at the end of your string of thoughts and words fail you can, in silence, know what it means, "To him be the glory forever!" And so be it.

Critical

A more critical reader could look at these lines another way. Not giving Paul the benefit of the doubt, which is my purpose here, one would conjecture that if a theologian was mistaken in his assumptions, sloppy in his use of scripture, and wrong about some points in his argument, what would his conclusion look like when he finally gave up? It might look like the jumble of astonishment and speculation we have in 11:33–36.

Postscript: The Error in First-Century Eschatology

The plain sense of the text of the Little Apocalypse in Matthew 24, Mark 13, and Luke 21 is that Jesus is warning his listeners of the trauma of the end of time because he expects it soon, in their lifetimes. He was wrong, which is an embarrassment for high Christologies. In much the same way Paul's teaching was eschatological and to that extent was misguided and in error.

In *Paul's Apocalyptic Gospel: The Coming Triumph of God*, J. Christiaan Beker connects Romans 11:25 ("I do not want you to be ignorant of this mystery") with 1 Corinthians 15:51 ("Listen, I tell you a mystery: We will not all sleep, but we will all be changed"):

This statement needs to be qualified in the light of Paul's occasional speech about a special end-time revelation (*mysterion*) which he has received (Rom. 11:25; 1 Cor. 15:51) and in the light of his expectation that certain events will take place before the end in a certain sequence. Thus Paul expects, "the full number of the Gentiles" to come in before the partial hardening of Israel is lifted (Rom. 11:25).[4]

That "We will not all sleep"—because time will end soon—was a revelation from the Lord that the apostle was wrong about. This error carries over in Romans 9—11 in his consideration of unbelieving Jews.

For Paul the signs of the resurrection of Jesus (1 Cor 15:20) and the coming of Gentiles into salvation (Rom 11:11) pointed to another miracle—the saving of all Israel (Rom 11:26). In his mind, this age of miracles was not to play out over two thousand years, a period of history that actually lay ahead. Instead Paul expected it all to end soon, in his readers' lifetime (1 Thess 4:15).

If Paul knew that Judaism was not going to be swallowed up by the victory of the church in the last days of his generation, would he have decided upon that solution to the split between Christianity and Judaism? If not, why do we stick with it after two thousand years of evidence of Judaism's ongoing vitality and validity? Paul's premise was faulty.

---

4. Beker, *Paul's Apocalytic Gospel*, 50–51.

7

Three Men at a Train Station

Torah Lesson: Leviticus 1:1–5:26
Beit HaTorah
March 16, 2013

Introduction

Getting right with God is at the heart of biblical religion, but in different ways for Jews and Christians. Messianic Judaism manifests a third possibility by relying on both election and justification. This meditation explores the differences in the three biblical faiths and argues with the presumption that there is only one set of tracks for the salvation train to God. It came to me in a dream.

Staying Acceptable

Nothing better illustrates the difference in the soteriologies of Christianity and Judaism than their trust in atonement for sin. Christians took the idea from the Jews and then reworked it, denigrating the Jewish belief in the process. But both atonements are efficacious.

The book of Leviticus begins with a picture of Jewish sacrifice. It is a picture of atonement. In the presence of the Lord, the worshipper brings an animal to be slaughtered. The layman does the killing here, not the priest. He does it in front of the priest, and the priest then takes the blood and sprinkles it—or dashes it—around the altar at the entrance to the tent of meeting. Leviticus 1:4 says, "[I]t will be accepted on your behalf to make atonement for you." Sounds like the ransom in the New Testament. But here the sinner, one of the elect, is already in a relationship with God.

The Elect Make Sacrifice

Another picture we have of this is right at the beginning of the book of Job where Job is being introduced as this worthy fellow. The book of Job does not begin with the meeting of the heavenly council where Satan shows up to talk to God about what he's found on earth. That starts at verse 1:6. The first five verses are about this man Job. I used to think he was not a Jew because it says, "There was a man in the land of Uz" (1:1 KJV), and wherever that was, it was outside of the land of Israel. But if you read on you discover Job making sacrifices to God according to the ritual described in the first nine verses of Leviticus. So he must have been a Jew in exile.

Let me read what it says about Job's animal sacrifices because it illustrates the important aspect of this atonement, which is that it is always a re-connection with God based upon a prior oneness with God. Job 1:4–5:

> His sons used to hold feasts in their homes on their birthdays, and they would invite their three sisters to eat and drink with them. When a period of feasting had run its course, Job would make arrangements for them to be purified. Early in the morning he would sacrifice a burnt offering for each of them, thinking, "Perhaps my children have sinned and cursed God in their hearts." This was Job's regular custom.

Now there was no tent of meeting out there in Uz, so the idea is that the people adapted the laws and rituals of animal sacrifice to suit their circumstances. The point here is that Job affected a reconciliation between his sons and daughters and God through continual sacrifices—in case they fell away the night before. He was not doing it to continually get his children saved. He was not doing it continually because the breakthrough to heaven never comes so he has to keep sacrificing over and over until, hopefully, one day it actually works. No! The children are already saved. They already have election. They start as Jews with an identity as part of the chosen people.

But they can curse God and fail in that privileged status. So the animal sacrifices are to re-connect, re-establish, re-store, and reconcile a relationship that was established by a prior covenant. A covenant they were born into as Jews. An election from eternity. If Job is a Jew, Job does not come to God daily to be made one with God for the first time every time. He comes for atonement—figuratively for *at-one-ment*—as an update in an ongoing saga, an ongoing story, the ongoing life of a Jew.

To restore a relationship is much different from beginning a relationship. When I was brought as an infant to the front of the church to be baptized, I was brought into a relationship. When I was brought as a teenager to a decision for Jesus Christ, I was brought into a relationship. I understood that apart from a faith decision for Christ I was lost. Without justification by faith, I had no home in heaven. That is not the experience of a Jew who comes to God in faith. A lost Jew who cursed God the night before is a bad son or bad daughter who is coming to his or her father God to make up, to reconcile, to restore the fellowship.

The glory of the Torah is that this is something we can do. We can find our way into the presence of God and make an act of sacrifice with contrition that will effect a change in the relationship. That is how much the Torah thinks of us. It is a promise that God will hear our prayers. If we follow the way of Moses, the way of Torah, the way of Leviticus, we can be righteous like Job. How did Job do it? He was blameless and upright, one who feared God and turned away from evil. Who turned toward God at the altar of sacrifice. The writer put that there for a reason. What do you suppose it was? I think it was to establish a relationship and to say that Job was pleasing to God.

God at the Altar

Now the picture in the New Testament is very different. Turn to 2 Corinthians 2:14–16. The subject here is not the worshipper. The actor here is God:

> But thanks be to God, who in Christ always leads us in triumphal procession, and through us spreads in every place the fragrance that comes from knowing him. For we are the aroma of Christ to God among those who are being saved and among those who are perishing. (NRSV)

I always misunderstood it to say we are a fragrance to God through Christ. I put it in a vertical dimension. But our participation here is actually all in the horizontal dimension. There is no ascent to heaven of this fragrance. The aroma is "in every place" on earth, "among those being saved and among those who are perishing." The name of the perfume is "Christ to God," not "Me to God" or "Us to God."

We have been saved by Christ, in other words. More precisely we have been saved by God's triumph in Christ, in God's act of making atonement for us in Christ's sacrifice—which sounds awfully familiar to those who have been ritually killing animals to worship God. But now Paul says that it is God at the altar as the actor, as the subject, as the one who is making a human sacrifice of his son Yeshua, effecting an atonement between humanity and God. This is Christianity.

Paul's Conclusion

Emil Brunner, an important theologian in the twentieth century, said the estrangement between humanity and God is like this:

> Two men board a train. One of them perhaps does something sensible, the other something stupid upon entering the coach. But as they look out, both notice that they have taken the wrong train and are going in the wrong direction. That one man was reasonable and the other stupid is a difference between these two men; it is a difference, however, that has no significance in relation to the fact that *both*, whatever their individual differences, are going in the wrong direction! This is what the Bible means by the word *sin*, the total perverse direction of our life, the tendency away from God. In this train all men are travelling, says the Apostle.[1]

For all the sin recorded in the Jewish scriptures it is never imagined as the consequence of being lost and without direction like the other nations who do not know God. Israel's very disobedience is in relationship to God. But the apostle Paul rejected Judaism. When the gate to heaven opened to him on the road to Damascus he only saw Yeshua, he did not see Yeshua and Abraham or Yeshua and Moses. He concluded that Abraham and Moses were not there in heaven, that apparently no Jews were in heaven apart from Christ's atonement. To use Emil Brunner's metaphor, Judaism became another train going in the wrong direction from God. In this respect the Jews were seen by Paul to be like every other people, every other nation. "God has shut up all in disobedience," he wrote (Rom 11:32).

---

1. Brunner, *Our Faith*, 41–42.

But following the way of Moses, the way of the Torah, is not like being shut up in disobedience. Moses was not shut up in disobedience. Torah observance is not the wrong train going in the wrong direction. It is the very opposite of that. Only people chosen by God can keep Torah. Doing it on your own, of your own initiative, is oxymoronic—it is just not able to be done that way. And if you are chosen by God you are, by that choice, put on the right train going in the right direction.

So there are the Jews and then, besides them, there are the Gentiles who do not get on the Torah train. They can get on other trains. One of those trains has Yeshua the Messiah, Jesus the Christ, as its chief engineer with Paul the apostle as its conductor. Like the way of the Jews, the way of the church is also a right way home. Two sets of tracks carry passengers to the same destination: the arms of God.

Messianic Dreams

I guess it was on a Wednesday night in August of 2004 that I had my own type of Damascus Road conversion experience, as a light from heaven shone down upon me at Clairvaux Farm as I was looking through the *Cecil Whig*. As I looked at the advertisement on the church page for Beit HaTorah a voice addressed me in my mind and heart and said "You are to go there." I know this as a fact. It is the truth of my salvation, the truth of my destiny.

After I started coming here, I started having dreams of importance about it, dreams I could remember enough to want to write down what I saw, what I was told. On October 10, 2004, I dreamed of reading the pages of *Biblical Literacy*, a book Yeshuel Creeger was teaching from in the hour prior to our service starting. In my dream, the pages were copies, bad copies, dark, unreadable copied pages, like when you don't cover the glass of the copy machine and you get a copy that is shaded in black. That was the image. It said to me that I needed more light, that I needed to persevere in this new thing in order to be able to learn it. December 4, 2004, I had a dream related to belonging to Messianic Judaism and my note about it says "in"—meaning I was in deep—and "so"—meaning therefore I was to get over it; and the line, "Perfect love casts out fear." I heard that in my dream. If I would start to love and forget about myself I would get over my anxiety. Five nights later on December 9, 2004, in my sleep, in my dreams, I heard a sentence of three words about becoming a Messianic Jew: "Another way home." I woke up and wrote it down: Another way home.

The Interpretation

I would like to think with you about the meaning of that dream and relate it to Emil Brunner's analogy of getting on a train going the wrong direction.

First of all, given that I was being addressed by another consciousness, by another voice not my own—I don't know what a psychologist would say about that but that is my experience—the one addressing me about another way home has to have had a sense of what is home. The dream tells me I am not presently at home—that my home is somewhere else. Only a consciousness that embraces both that other place and my current situation could speak of another way home. The best sense I can make of it is that the voice came from that other place. The voice knows that place and knows me and knows that it is there that I truly belong.

To know what is in that other place is a vast amount of knowledge unavailable to me. I don't even have a sense of not being at home. I was perfectly content the night the voice told me to come here to this synagogue. I had no crying need to change my life, to change my faith, to change the terms of my salvation. In 2004, I was in the fourth year of a pastorate to two churches in Delaware City and Port Penn and I was doing a pretty good job. They liked me, and I liked them. The preaching was going well, the visitations were going well, the plans for the annual church bazaar were going well. I was the president of the board of directors of Meeting Ground, a very successful ministry to homeless persons. That is what I was doing out at Clairvaux Farm, volunteering for my agency. I had been happily married twenty-three years that month. My son would soon be a sophomore in high school, on a scholarship. My daughter had graduated high school in the spring and had moved on campus as a student at the nearby University of Delaware. She had a boyfriend from high school who was also at the university. They were in love.

To tell me I was not at home in this life was a strange thing. But that is what I learned in my dream: my new faith was another way home. Who could tell me that but a voice from heaven who knew both home and me—who knew the gulf between them, who knew the depth and height and width of the separation between where I was lying in my bed and where I was destined to arrive at? I was going to have to go on a "way." The one speaking to me, to say what was said, had to know that way and that I was suited for it and that it was suited for me and that the beginning point and the ending point were connected by it.

Different Sets of Tracks

More than that, the phrase "Another way home" carries the knowledge of different ways home. It tells me there is the one way—Messianic Judaism. But it also tells me that the way of Messianic Judaism is not the only way home. It is another way, an additional way, home. There are separate sets of tracks leading to the arms of God. There is not one train at the salvation station. If that was the case my dream would have been "The way home." I did not hear that. I heard "Another way home." So the divine consciousness addressing me in my sleep with enough power and purpose to carry over into my awakened consciousness had to know that there are at least two ways home: two or more.

As one who has not been shaken from a biblical faith, I now say there are these three ways home in the revelation of sacred scripture: the way of the Torah for Jews, the way of Christ for the church, and the way of Torah and Yeshua the Messiah for Messianic Jews. Messianic Judaism is not one kind of Judaism like Orthodox, Conservative, Reformed, or Reconstructionist Judaisms. It is another way home. Messianic Judaism is not one kind of baptized membership in the Body of Christ. It is not through baptism at all. It is another way home.

Divisive Christian Words

Here I am on the same ground as the apostle Paul when he writes in 1 Thessalonians 2:15 that the Jews, "who killed the Lord Jesus and the prophets and also drove us out. They displease God. . . ." That is a description of divided ground. That is a division between "us" and "them." Paul is saying to the Thessalonians, *we* are the ones who please God. *We* are the ones who confess Jesus as Lord. *They* are the other ones. *They* are the enemy.

My dream was also about division on earth, about divided ground, about different sets of tracks. "Another way home" implies that out there are the other ones. The ones you, Jeff, used to belong to—the Christians. Now you are joining the Messianic Jews with another faith, another life, another identity. Not Christian. So I am okay with Paul's adversarial assumption. It is his hate speech that offends.

Why does Judaism get such bad treatment in the New Testament? Why do the Jews have to be wrong for the Christians to be right?

The writer of the book of Acts dramatizes Paul's divisiveness with a story about his time of ministry in Corinth. Turn to Acts 18:5–6. In verse 5, we learn of Paul's devotion to proving to the Jews of Corinth that Jesus was the Christ. Verse 6 records what followed:

> But when they opposed Paul and became abusive, he shook out his clothes in protest and said to them, "Your blood be upon your own heads! I am innocent of it. From now on I will go to the Gentiles.

Wow. What does he mean when he tells the Jews, "Your blood be upon your own heads"? He is telling them to die. It is a saying from 2 Samuel and 1 Kings that introduces executions. The sense is, "Your own blood, from out of your own body, be on your own head." Paul is saying, "Die Jews." Then he adds, "I am innocent"—that is, I am clean from the guilt and responsibility of your deaths. This is hate speech to Jews in the book of Acts.

Chosen With Faults

John Calvin writes these words of commentary on Paul's threat in Acts 18:6:

> He denounceth to them vengeance, because they be without excuse. For they can shift no part of their fault from themselves.[2]

That is a classic Christian outlook on those Jews: "They can shift no part of their fault from themselves." All those animal sacrifices can do nothing to shift any part of their fault from themselves. Apart from God's triumph in Christ, apart from that act of atonement, they are just being religious in a way that changes nothing in regards to their fault.

But that is not what the Jews say about themselves. Of course they deal with faults that need to be atoned for. The Hebrew scriptures are full of fault-finding. The Jews know their faults better than anyone. You know Paul was a Hebrew among Hebrews just by the way he sees so much wrong with them. He kvetches—about being Jewish.

But just as they know themselves so well they know their God so well. They know to whom they belong. What the Jews say about themselves is that the Lord spoke to Moses and Moses spoke the words of the Torah—the five books of Moses. Their idea of atonement is not the Christians' idea. They are not sacrificing to establish a relationship, to enter in to a covenant. The men's penises tell them they are already in a covenant. They come to God for atonement knowing God has made them the Jews, the chosen people. They are saved by election, not by any justification. So this fault, no part of which they can shift from themselves, is not damnation. It does not cut

---

2. Calvin, "Calvin's Commentaries: Acts 18," section 6.

them off from God. It does not require a new basis for salvation. It does not require another way home. Sure they have faults. But so do the Christians. So do the Messianic Jews. We all have faults that can only be lifted from us by God's grace. But we do not die from them. We pray for God's mercy. That mercy, God's *hesed*, comes to us from heaven when we are in a covenantal relationship with the Father.

Multiple Covenants

The upshot of my message is that Messianic Judaism is by both election and by justification. If Judaism is one way home by election and Christianity is one way home by justification, Messianic Judaism is another way home by both election and justification. Some Christian theologians tell us this is true in Christianity—that there is prevenient grace before justifying grace. Christians also understand themselves as the children of Abraham. But they find their election in Christ. Messianic Jews have an election in the covenant of the Torah. It is not the same as being elected in Messiah Yeshua. It is another election that leads us into Torah observance. We believe God acted in giving us the Torah just as God acted in sacrificing his son on the execution stake. The Christians do not believe in that correspondence and other Jews do not either. Only Messianic Jews have both an election in Torah and a justification in the blood of Messiah.

So Emil Brunner got it wrong back in 1936 when he said, "Two men board a train"—both on the wrong train going in the wrong direction. He misjudges that there is just one right direction and only one train on one set of tracks going the right way. The way I read my Bible there are three possibilities for getting home. One home for us all, but three tracks laid down. Saul did not see Moses when he glimpsed heaven on the road to Damascus but that just means heaven is bigger than can be seen in a glimpse. Moses is up there. Yeshua is up there. So is the apostle Paul, along with many, many other Jews. So may we all be by the grace of God in his triumph through the Torah and by the grace of God in his triumph through Yeshua. Amen.

Discussion C: A Place for Jews in God's Plan and Purpose for this World

Dual-Covenant Theology

Franz Rosenzweig (1886–1929) reflected hard upon the relationship between Christianity and Judaism. He once observed,

> Christianity acknowledges the God of the Jews, not as God but as "the Father of Jesus Christ." Christianity itself cleaves to the "Lord" because it knows that the Father can be reached only through him. With his church, he remains as the "Lord" for all time, until the end of the world, but then he will cease to be the Lord, and he too will be subject to the Father who will, on this day, be all in all. We are all wholly agreed as to what Christ and his church mean to the world; no one can reach the Father save through him.
>
> No one can reach the Father! But the situation is quite different for one who does not have to reach the Father because he is already with him. And this is true of the people of Israel (though not of individual Jews).[1]

Emmanuel Levinas (1906–1995) was another Jewish philosopher who tried to make sense of Judaism to the Western world. He wrote,

---

1. Rosenzweig, "The Church and the Synagogue," 341.

Discussion C: A Place for Jews in God's Plan and Purpose for this World

> *Human truth, both Christian and Jewish, is verification.* It consists in risking one's life by living it in reply to the Revelation—that is to say, in reply to the Love of God.[2]

On June 9, 1991, Pope John Paul II (1920–2005) delivered these words in a farewell address in Warsaw at the end of his fourth tour of Poland as pontiff:

> Meetings with representatives of Jewish communities are a constant element of my apostolic journeys. This fact has its significance, because it underlines a unique *community of faith* which *connects sons of Abraham*, followers of the religion of Moses and the prophets, with those who also *recognize Abraham as their "father in faith"* (John 8:39) and accept in Christ, "Son of Abraham and Son of David" (Matt. 1:1), the whole extremely rich *legacy of Moses and the prophets* too.[3]

These reflections by Rosenzweig, Levinas, and Pope John Paul II are sincere efforts at reconciling the two experiences of God that underlie Christianity and Judaism. In that search for common ground the third religion of Messianic Judaism is now relevant and helpful. What is unhelpful is denying an experience of God by any of the three parties to biblical faith. This is being done by some Christians, by some Jews, and by some Messianic Jews. Respectively, they are not interested in finding common ground but instead define themselves in opposition to the faith of others. Waking up everyday to defend an exclusive relationship to God and the Bible is inspiring to some people.

A World Without Jews?

The Messianic Jews of Beit HaTorah, on the other hand, do not limit the power of prayer, the ministry of angels, the revelation of the Bible, the love of God or the kingdom of God to our own faith and practice. Our way of interpreting scripture is right for us but we do not therefore denounce others for reading the Bible differently and finding themselves addressed therein. Rabbi Abraham Joshua Heschel saw through to its logical conclusion the mission by some Christians to evangelize Jews and convert them:

> The mission to the Jews is a call to betray . . . the sacred history of their people. Very few Christians seem to comprehend what

---

2. Bell, *Seeds of the Spirit*, 92.
3. John Paul II, "To the Representatives."

is morally and spiritually involved in supporting such activities. We are Jews as we are men. The alternative to our existence as Jews is spiritual suicide, extinction. It is not a change into something else. Judaism has allies but no substitutes. . . .

Gustave Weigel spent the last evening of his life in my study at the Jewish Theological Seminary. We opened our hearts to one another in prayer and contrition and spoke of our own deficiencies, failures, hopes. At one moment I posed the question: Is it really the will of God that there be no more Judaism in the world? Would it really be the triumph of God if the scrolls of the Torah would no more be taken out of the Ark and the Torah no more read in the Synagogue, our ancient Hebrew prayers, in which Jesus himself worshipped, no more recited, the Passover Seder no more celebrated in our lives, the law of Moses no more observed in our homes? Would it really be *ad majorem Dei gloriam* to have a world without Jews?[4]

The Messianic Jewish movement is currently divided between those who share a vision of pluralism or "dual covenants" and those who are evangelical and deny that God wills the continuation and prosperity of the Jewish religion alongside Christianity and Messianic Judaism.

By Grace and Mercy

Read Romans 11.

Paul has the zeal of a convert and sees the world in the stark terms of there being just two kinds of people: the saved and the unsaved (v. 14). But he knows too much truth to make that simplistic view stick. He repeatedly qualifies God's rejection of the Jews (v. 15) who do not believe in Yeshua as Messiah. See verses 1–2.

What keeps getting in the way is God's election of Israel: "their own olive tree" (v. 24). Like Abraham Heschel, Paul cannot see a world without Jews. Look at the paradox of verse 28. Two opposites are both affirmed as true. The Jews are the enemy of God's people and their gospel *and* they are loved by God on an entirely different basis, their election. On the one hand (v. 29), "God gifts and his call are irrevocable"; they cannot be invalidated. The Jews are valid. On the other hand (v. 31), "so they too have now become disobedient in order that they too may now receive mercy." He does not see that God's original choice of the Jews—that irrevocable call—was by mercy:

---

4. Heschel, "Mission to the Jews," 110–11.

because mercy and grace came to him through Jesus. Though Paul chose not to, it is possible to affirm both experiences.

Questions

1. In reading the New Testament, should Messianic Jews identify with the Christians or the Jews—as a part of the wild olive tree or the cultivated olive tree (Rom 11:24)?

2. There may be no one more invested in the Christian way of salvation than the Pope, and yet Pope John Paul II described a family connection creating a common community with Catholics and Jews in Poland. What assumption is he making that evangelical Christians do not make?

3. Emmanuel Levinas's quote suggests that our assertions about whose side God is on and what is God's truth are unverifiable apart from the lives we live. Words and ideas become true through us; they are not dropped into the world from heaven without fingerprints. Have you ever seen God's truth in the life of someone of another religion?

8

Correspondence with Rabbi Adam Yisroel

Introduction

I have discovered over the years that there is variety in Messianic Jewish congregations. The label covers an array of worship practices, leadership styles, congregational priorities, and expectations for membership. At first I casually adopted those at Beit HaTorah as normative, which was unrealistic.

One of my first visits to another Messianic ministry was to the Mikveh Yisrael Messianic Congregation in Erie, Pennsylvania. It was led by Rabbi Adam Yisroel who observes an Orthodox Messianic Judaism for himself and with members of his congregation. They sit around a large table on Shabbat and study Torah before having refreshments. In my first efforts at introducing Messianic Judaism, I tried to have it both ways and sometimes spoke of Jesus as divine as well as human. I sent this book of lessons to the rabbi, and he seized upon the references in it to the divinity of Yeshua. With permission I have reprinted his letter here, from February 15, 2012, addressed to my Hebrew name Daniel, followed by an edited version of my response.

He offers an emphatic exposition of New Testament passages on monotheism. My reflections that follow tell how Messianic Jews can take the scriptures of two other religions and create a third one. Combining Jesus with Torah observance is a new possibility in God's plan and purpose. It involves respect for the beliefs of Jews and Christians along with a need to respectfully differ in our understanding of the same God of the Bible.

> Shalom Daniel,
>
> I apologize for not writing sooner, but I have been busy writing my own book. It has taken up all my spare time. However I did read a great deal of the lessons that you sent to me. From what I read I see that we are not in agreement as to who Y'shua is. *We believe he is the Savior, the Mashiach, Son of G-d, King of Yisroel, sinless Lamb of G-d, the one sent from G-d as a mediator between G-d and man but we do not believe he is G-d or ever claimed to be G-d.* You must consider the verses that are very clear about this. After Y'shua's resurrection and he was speaking to Thomas he said "I go to my Father and your Father *to my G-d and your G-d."* To which I would have to ask, Can G-d have a G-d?

False Doctrine

> In Revelation 3:12 Y'shua calls G-d *his G-d* no less than 4 times. If G-d can have a G-d would that not make two gods? And would not the god that Y'shua served be a greater god then himself? This is pure polytheism. We believe in One indivisible G-d who is the Eternal and who even Y'shua called *the only true G-d* in John 17:3 where he says *"This is eternal life that they might know you the only true G-d and Y'shua HaMashiach whom you sent."* It is very clear that Y'shua knew who G-d was and he did not claim to be that G-d.
>
> Also there are some very clear statements from the Scripture that state that G-d can not sin nor can he be tempted with sin yet Y'shua was tempted 40 days and nights in the wilderness. The Scripture also says that *G-d raised Y'shua from the dead.* If G-d was still alive somewhere in the universe so that he could raise himself from the dead then our salvation has not been secured because G-d never really died.
>
> I could go on all night with these examples but I would hope that you would read a book that might answer all the questions. It is *The Doctrine of the Trinity: Christianity's Self-Inflicted Wound* by *Anthony Buzzard.* You can purchase it from Amazon. If you wish to talk to me more about this I would be willing to do that. If you wish to sever ties I understand that as well. I hope

that you choose to investigate this more. Go on the internet and look up the 'origins of the doctrine of the Trinity' and you will see that it's history cannot be found in the Bible but only in the doctrines of men.

Just a couple other verses to think about. 1 Cor. 1:3, "*Blessed be the G-d, even the Father of our lord Y'shua HaMashiach.*" Acts 2:22, "*You men of Israel hear these words: Y'shua HaMashiach, a man approved of G-d among you by miracles and wonders and signs, which G-d did through him in the midst of you, as you yourselves know.*" As you can see for yourself he was a man approved by G-d, whom G-d did these things through. It does not say that he was G-d. There is one mediator between G-d and man: the *man* Mashiach Y'shua.

Please read these verses, get the book and don't be afraid to do the research. It will be the best thing you ever did. I am willing to talk if you have any questions . . . . The answering machine is always on so wait for me to get to the phone if I'm home. If not leave your number and I'll call you back.

Rabbi Adam

A Much Needed Corrective

Dear Rabbi Adam,

Shalom to you! I knew I wanted to send you a copy of my manuscript because you would read it and take it seriously. You and I could talk over these matters for a long time. I have decided to put my ideas in writing. I find it not only clarifies my thinking but prompts it further. Thank you for guiding my thinking with your written response. I looked up the verses and did some research related to Anthony Buzzard.

In your citations from the New Testament you have given me a much-needed corrective to the impression I gave that Messianic Jews can be trinitarian. I agree with you that they cannot be. Messianic Jews are not a part of the Christian church. We are our own religion. We are Bible-based, but are not Christians nor are we traditional Jews.

Right now it seems like there are two choices in regard to believing in the God of the Bible: Judaism and Christianity. The old and the new. The Bible is a creation of the church so everyone using the New Testament associates themselves with the church and Christianity. Some may consider the historical church apostate and themselves the true followers of Jesus Christ. But there is no one out there except Messianic Jews saying:

- that you can follow Messiah Jesus and not be a Christian or in the church;
- that you can receive the baptism of the Holy Spirit and not be a Christian or in the church;
- that you can embrace the New Testament as holy scripture and not be a Christian or in the church.

A New Paradigm

I think of Messianic Judaism as a third son among the offspring of the God of the Bible. Right now common perceptions in Western academia, society, religious culture, and conventional wisdom are arranged around God's two offspring: Judaism and Christianity. I want to shatter that paradigm with the introduction of a third offspring. That is the purpose of my authorship.

To shatter the paradigm I need to undermine Christianity's claim to exclusiveness—the claim that the New Testament has only one rightful owner, the church universal. Rival faiths in The Church of Jesus Christ of Latter-day Saints and in the Jehovah's Witnesses have not tried to be a third biblical religion. They both take the New Testament from the church and still agree with the paradigm of two offspring from the God of the Bible. They each would displace the church universal as the true New Testament faith. Each has a vision to be the authentic second offspring of God after the Jews. Some Messianic Jews buy into this sort of vision for themselves. Some do it by wanting to take the place of the church, others do it by wanting to take the place of the Jews. My book about a new hermeneutic and soteriology alongside the church's might as well be titled *The Third Son* or *The Third Daughter*.

In my message "Renewed Fear" (see Chapter 12), I make much of the difference between "a new covenant" and "a renewed covenant." This corresponds with the notion of a double movement of covenantal commitment (developed in Discussion B). Messianic Jews are doing to the Christians what the first Christians did to the Jews: reading their scriptures in a new and different way and claiming for this a new mantle of authority. "Covenant" and "testament" are synonymous. Christians coined the term "old covenant" for scriptures that had never been known by that name. Messianic Jews have coined the term "renewed covenant"/"renewed testament" and should now apply it to scriptures that have never been known by that name. That is how you introduce yourself as a third offspring.

Judaism was first, Christianity was second. A third biblical religion necessarily follows in the steps of the second. The key to Christianity's legitimacy as an offspring of God is the clever two-sided conviction of Paul that it was the God of Judaism acting in Jesus Christ, on the one hand; on the other hand, that this act was something new and different and final *and* it also subsumed and set aside every other covenantal act of Israel's God. You do not have to agree to both sides of the "*and*" in that sentence. I am saying that you can believe that Yeshua's life, death, and resurrection were something new, different, and final in God's plan and purpose *and not* believe that it subsumed and set aside God's other covenants with the Jews.

To the Jews, then, I am saying that Messianic Jews can believe and follow the Torah and the covenants God made with the Jews *and* add an additional covenant that does not subsume the earlier ones.

The Move to Inclusivity

Christianity and the church needed that exclusivity to establish themselves as an offspring of God other than the Jews: a second son by a new covenant. I am now called as a third son by that same covenant together with the earlier ones. Christians could have been Messianic Jews if they had wanted to be. Instead they went with the apostle Paul and an exclusive, new covenant in Jesus Christ. Thus in the twenty-first century God reveals that his grace is greater than Christians have known because it embraces Torah-observant believers in Christ as well as non-Torah-observant believers in Christ.

For Messianic Jews and Gentiles, Paul's choice between justification by the law (Torah) and justification by faith is a false choice. We embrace both. So in our religion we respect Torah observance as a means of grace. Christianity does not. Christianity adds religious features we do not have: church history and theology, baptism and other sacraments, and its holidays. Every sort of Christian goes to Good Friday and Easter services. Why not also attend the seder at Passover, as prescribed in the Old Testament? Because it makes no Christian sense.

Messianic Judaism Does Not Correct or Displace Judaism

To be the third son in God's family it is necessary to both reject the exclusivism of Christianity and to embrace the legitimacy of Judaism. That sounds like an obvious affirmation for a Messianic Jew to make but not if you are evangelical. Traditional Jews are alert to this denial. They ask, how can you be "Messianic" and still be a Jew? This criticism is directed at the evangelical Messianic Jews who would try to establish themselves as the truest Jews, the most complete.

In his book, *Yeshua the Messiah*, Messianic Rabbi David Chernoff is willing to devalue the Torah, Moses, and rabbinic Judaism in order to have Yeshua. He compartmentalizes: primacy to Yeshua and secondary standing to the old covenants.[1] Except in the practice of his congregation he also wants to correct the church's ways and not be Christian. Then primacy goes to the Jewish calendar and customs—Saturday Sabbaths, Jewish holidays, Jewish lectionary, Hebrew names, etc.—and secondary standing to church history and Christian traditions.

How could Jews be offended at this? Because it accepts the premise of Judaism being a secondary revelation of God but retains all the outward signs and practices. It accepts the premise that a believer in the God of Israel is either a Christian or a Jew—and the Messianic Jews are not the Christians. They must therefore displace the Jews. They must reject a traditional Jewish identity that gives primacy to itself as being chosen by God. The question is, Can you be a Jew if other Jews say you are not a Jew? Arguably, the reply is no. Which is why Messianic Judaism today is basically a sect of Christianity.

Newer Than New

I am saying that there can be another kind of genuine Jew. So my greatest challenge will not come from the Christians but from traditional Jews. Can the Torah observance and Torah study of Messianic Jews count as authentic? Can Messianic Jews call themselves Jews while separate from Talmudic Judaism? Perhaps they can if I shatter the paradigm of the two offspring of God and leave the Talmudic Jews alone to do what they have always done. This would be to their advantage because in the introduction of a third offspring of the God of the Bible I am doing away with the top-down orientation in the two-offspring paradigm. That is, I am elevating Judaism in the process. I also do away with the new-old orientation in the two-offspring paradigm. What was "old" is suddenly newer than "new."

How will it be done? Not by redefining "Christian" and not by redefining "Jew" but by redefining "Messianic." (This is the thrust of Discussion D.) Traditional Jews might accept the Messianic Jews calling themselves "Jews" as long as they are not really Christians. Look at the mystical Kabbalistic tradition of the Zohar in Judaism. Devotees embrace esoteric ideas having

---

[1] Chernoff writes, "The responsibility for keeping the 'Mitzvot' (Commandments) was on us. The problem as that we could not obey them and kept transgressing God's law over and over again. Every time we sinned we needed to get another animal sacrifice for a 'covering.' And if the sin was willful and not in ignorance, there was no sacrifice available at all! Obviously, something greater was needed. Something more *permanent* had to be done about our spiritual condition." Chernoff, *Yeshua the Messiah*, 67.

little resemblance to common interpretations of Moses, the Prophets, and the Writings; still, Talmudic Jews acknowledge them as fellow Jews. Judaism is an elastic belief system. But it will not allow itself to be hijacked into oblivion by Jewish Christianity. If you let the incarnation of God in the door very soon it will be all Christianity.

What have I done? Redefine the "Christ" in "Jesus Christ." Explicitly reject Christianity. I have made room for a third biblical religion. All the covenants have equal standing, whether in Genesis or in Exodus or in Romans. Messiahs are, in essence, de-emphasized so that their titles are best rendered with lower-case letters. Yeshua is a messiah in Messianic Judaism. He is the Messiah in Christianity. As a Messianic believer I want Jesus, but I cannot take with him everything the New Testament says about him. As a Messianic believer, I consider the New Testament to be scripture, but I do not give every verse equal weight, just as Christians feel free to devalue some verses in their reading of the Old Testament.

In redefining "Christ" and rejecting Christianity, I am rejecting the third part of John 1:1, that "the Word was God." But two out of three isn't bad: "In the beginning was the Word and the Word was with God." Rabbi Creeger's teaching that Yeshua was the embodiment of the Torah or the incarnation of it sounds similar to the prologue to the Gospel of John, the highest Christology in the New Testament, but there is a line of divine incarnation we dare not cross. Fortunately in the New Testament there are a number of lines drawn about the uniqueness of Jesus that we can cross—fortunate in the sense that recognition of what God was doing in Yeshua should not be limited to the highest Christology. We are saved through multiple covenants, including the covenant God made through Jesus Christ/Yeshua HaMashiach. We understand that covenant differently than the church does, and consequently, we understand the way God was in Christ differently than the church does.

Scriptural and Sound

It must be stressed that our belief in Messiah Yeshua is scriptural and sound even as it differs from the Christian belief. We embrace the whole of the New Testament even while de-emphasizing some passages and emphasizing others in the way of our own religion. So when asked, "Do you believe in Jesus?" we become confident in our affirmation by being aware of the different pictures the New Testament shows us. Paul has a heavenly vision. The book of Revelation has another heavenly vision. The synoptic gospels show different sides to Jesus while sharing the assumption of miracles and resurrection.

The Gospel of John is a fourth portrayal of Jesus. In creating the canon of the New Testament the church voted to include all these portraits and leave it to believers of each generation to discern their individual and common truth.

Messianic Judaism must follow this collective, canonical path. We insist on the whole canonical New Testament, the whole Bible, as our scripture. But we are not Christians. What counts as evidence in the study of the messiah or Christology? What counts as evidence as to who Yeshua is? How we go about answering these questions determines the possible answers.

We go about answering these questions, first of all, as Jews answer them. This is what separates our conclusions about Yeshua from the church's teaching about him. Jews know that God is one. That should be the Messianic Jewish paradigm. That is how we view the world, how we interpret reality, how we read scripture: monotheisitically. The audacious claim of Messianic Judaism is that the Jesus of the New Testament fits our paradigm. That makes some verses difficult for us. But Christians and Jews also know about difficult Bible verses.

Emphasis and De-emphasis

We must not reopen the canon and pick and choose. The whole New Testament counts as the body of scripture we hold on to as a revelation of God. This does not bind us to Christianity, just as the church's use of the Old Testament does not bind it to Judaism. With inspiration from above we are making new applications of New Testament truths by reading with a new focus in mind. Some verses that Christians leave in the shadows we bring into the light. Some verses Christianity lifts up we must de-emphasize. But we insist on the Bible as our book.

The chief end of my efforts in writing this lengthy reply on top of the lesson book I sent you is to establish a plain meaning for the sentence, "Messianic Jews are the Jews who believe Jesus was a messiah." Thank you for pushing me further toward the achievement of that goal. Best wishes to you, your family, and your congregation. I value our friendship.

Grace and Peace,

Jeffrey W. Dandoy (Daniel)

9

Beyond Complaint

Torah Lesson: Exodus 13:17—17:16
Beit HaTorah
January 26, 2013

Introduction

James A. Sanders entitled a book of sermons *God Has a Story Too*. Religion, soteriology, and the Bible are not only human matters, they are initiatives of God. So with the story of Israel's march through the wilderness. It is God's story too, and he has an agenda he is accomplishing, with implications for us. Being Messianic is one way to meet God's expectations as he makes his move in the twenty-first century.

A New Start

It is a remarkable set of circumstances when you think about how many hopes and dreams accompanied the walk of freedom. Everyone must have had long-held thoughts and images about what freedom would be like, how they would live, where they would live, what they would do. People do not just long for a better life. They long for a certain view from the front porch, for a certain job, for a certain kind of house, for a certain meal, for a certain reunion, for a certain piece of land, for a certain education for their children, for a certain way of relaxing, for a certain time to dance and to sing and to celebrate. All these runaway slaves knew was that they were going to a mountain to worship. Not to live there but to encounter God.

What God and Moses are doing in this is giving these people a task that they can accomplish by themselves. They have no track record of success. All they have known is the lash. They never worked for themselves. They never had a chance to do something on their own. This is their chance. They are to meet God at this mountain. To do it they have to walk. To do it they have to overcome their insecurity and fear. They have to learn to trust a leader. They have to be more than Egyptian property—more than victims, more than their pain.

Two Versions of the Story

Now we have God's word that these Hebrew slaves stood up for themselves at one point. The slaves themselves, when they are runaway and scared, will deny this—deny they ever stood up for themselves. In both cases we just have to take each one's word for it because the storyteller never really says what happened that got God and these people together. In Exodus 3:7-9, HaShem tells Moses,

> I have heard them crying out because of their slave drivers . . .
> And now the cry of the Israelites has reached me, and I have
> seen the way the Egyptians are oppressing them.

We must presume, because the text does not say, that these were cries for help and not just cries of emotion and pain. We do not know what words the slaves cried out and, at this point, it does not seem to matter. These people are really suffering and they need help. But turn to Exodus 14:12. There we read, "Didn't we say to you in Egypt, 'Leave us alone; let us serve the Egyptians'?"

They say that they told God and Moses to let them alone. They did not cry for help. They were "serving" the Egyptians. Now just as we do not have a record of what God heard in those cries he described to Moses neither do we have a record of this conversation the runaway slaves claim to have had before the Passover. So who really is responsible for this relationship of people and their liberator is a mystery. God says the people initiated it. They stood up and cried out to him. The people say it was all God's idea. They told him, "No thanks, leave us alone."

A Covenant Partnership

Looking at it again from our higher perspective of knowing what is coming, I suspect the recollection of the people is more accurate than God's memory of being asked. Because God is on the lookout for a people to whom he can give the divine revelation of the Torah. As an observant Jew knows, that is a burden. Jews and Messianic Jews are a type of Amos: "burden bearers." Slaves from Egypt may have said they had had enough burden bearing.

God would not be deterred. God is seeking a covenant partner, and that is what the nation of runaway slaves ends up becoming. This outcome suggests God proposed the relationship, and the people began by turning him down. They were looking for a date—a way out of Cairo. God was looking for a marriage partner. He had a prenuptial agreement prepared. He was going to hand it to Moses at the mountain. God was ready. He was on the move. He was ready to change the world, to change history, to be more for humanity than he had ever been. He had recruited Moses. All he needed was a people who would follow. And he says they cried out to him for help.

If that is the case, this is the only covenant in the Bible initiated on the human side. When you think of God's covenant with Abraham, of God's covenant with Noah, of God's covenant with David, and of the new covenant God made through Messiah Yeshua—God is the initiator. It is always grace, prevenient grace. Abraham, David, the Jews of the first century in Galilee and in Jerusalem—they could not bring God down from heaven with their cries, with their prayers, with their need; even with their sin. God sent his angels to Abraham and Sarah. God sent his angels to Zechariah and to Mary and to Joseph. With the possible exception of Jacob pressing his angel, no one in the Bible ever directs God. No one of us can really say to God, "Let's make a deal."

God is not an idol. Idols always say yes. God is not in the business of granting three wishes like an Arabian genie. God does not necessarily come when he is summoned. Except that he will honor his covenants. He will keep his promises. But a promise from God is not the fulfillment of a wish. Instead it is an act of his sovereign lordship. It is a manifestation of his glory. It is a fulfillment of what he has already begun in calling you into his covenant.

God Saw Something In Them

What we see in today's Torah portion is God on the move, sweeping this people along until they can catch up with him. The Torah—the Bible—is God's story. How many of us want to be caught up in God's story? What if that means, as it did for Abraham, for Noah, and for these Israelites in Egypt, that to be a part of God's story you must walk away from everything you know and start over somewhere new? What if to be a part of God's story you must take real risks and make real sacrifices and give up real freedoms in order to do things another way than you ever imagined? It is not easy saying yes to God when you do not really know what you are saying yes to.

All that the Israelites said yes to was to be free and to worship God at that mountain. The biblical records claims that they did not even go for that. Instead, they say they were compelled by Moses to leave. They claim they just wanted to be left alone with what they knew: their life in Egypt. But God saw something in them that was the potential to be better than that. God saw in them a people he wanted to covenant with, a people he wanted to belong to. "I am the God of your father, the God of Abraham, the God of Isaac, and the God of Jacob" (Exod 3:6), he told Moses at their first meeting. He introduced himself by way of his connection to the Jews.

Here is another reason I believe the Israelites when they say they told God, "No. Leave us alone." That takes chutzpah. God likes that. These Jews were tough. Throw away their children, and they still show up for work. Take away their straw, and they still make the bricks. The writer of the book of Exodus plays down their virtues and emphasizes their vulnerabilities; and they come to be known as a "stiff-necked people." But that kind of assertiveness cuts both ways, doesn't it? God did not choose a subservient people who would never question him, never fight him, never stand up to him. I think he knew that from the start.

God does not mind your sass. God is not afraid of your honest doubts. Elohim knows the way of the Torah is the way of sacrifice and that sometimes sacrificing for God can be hard. Just remember this: it is not about you. That is one of the key truths in Rick Warren's book, *The Purpose-Driven Life*. In figuring out your life begin by understanding that it is not about you. Rick Warren offers this prayer for the New Year:

> Father, as I begin this journey, help me to realize that building my life around myself instead of you will only lead to emptiness and meaninglessness. I was made by you and for you, and I want to discover my purpose in you.[1]

---

1. Warren, *Purpose-Driven Journal*, "Day 1."

The Jews were the first to uncover this truth. Before Christians were discovering their purpose in God, the Jews had been doing it for thousands of years by Torah observance. If there is anything in this world that communicates the lesson, "It is not about you," it has to be Torah observance.

A Pattern Emerges

To illustrate this I would like to walk through the story of Israel's wilderness experience by highlighting the verses and episodes that speak of the people's complaint against God. I want to observe not only the cycle of complaint but also a pattern in regards to Torah observance that might give us some insight into our faithfulness to the Torah.

Earlier we looked at the episode of thirst in Exodus 17:1–4, in which the mob looked liked it wanted to stone Moses. The outcome was deliverance with water springing forth from the rock at Horeb.

Turn backwards from there one chapter to Exodus 16:2–3, where the same struggle went on: "In the desert the whole community grumbled against Moses and Aaron" (v. 2). Everyone was hungry. The outcome is divine deliverance when God sends manna.

Turn back just a few verses from chapter 16 to Exodus 15:22–24, where the people are three days without water. At 15:24 it says, "So the people grumbled against Moses." The outcome of that episode was fresh water to drink. The people are miraculously delivered.

These passages of complaint and deliverance in Exodus 15—17 all take place after the crossing of the Red Sea, which was another great deliverance that came in response to the people's complaint. Look at Exodus 14:10-12. This is where they say they never wanted to be part of this, that they told God to leave them alone. "What have you done to us?" they ask their leader. Then Moses opened a way where there was no way and set the people free.

That is the first half of the cycle of complaint in a pattern of call and response: the people cry out, and God hears their cry and delivers them. Now I want to turn to the book of Numbers, chapter 11. The book of Exodus takes us a far as Mount Sinai where God reveals the Torah to the people of Israel. Numbers tells us what happened afterward. Numbers, beginning at 11:1–3, shows us that the cycle of complaint continued. But the pattern of call and response changed.

Look at Numbers 11:1–3: "Now when the people complained in the hearing of the LORD about their misfortunes, the Lord heard it" (NRSV). Familiar ground so far. We are not certain if it was thirst or hunger or something else that caused them to complain. But they cried out again, and the

Lord heard. This time, instead of an outcome of deliverance, we have an outcome of judgment: "[T]he Lord heard it and his anger was kindled" (NRSV). One time before the Red Sea, two times on the other side of the Red Sea, three times complaining, four times complaining—and God always comes through. Now, on the far side of Mount Sinai, the pattern has changed.

Now when they complain, God shows them his anger. First in Numbers 11:1. Again, a few verses later at Numbers 11:4–9, people begin to crave meat that they do not have. All this manna: morning, noon, and night. Verse 4: "The Israelites also wept again" (NRSV). This would be the sixth time. But who is counting? Turn the page to the end of chapter, to Numbers 11:31–33, and you find an outcome of deliverance but also another kindling of the wrath of Adonai. This kind of response is new.

Finally, for one more episode, turn to Numbers 14:1–2: crying and weeping and complaining. Further down at verse 10 they are ready again to stone Moses. The first time that happened, back in the book of Exodus, God simply got Moses out of a difficult situation by bringing water from the rock. That was the end of it. Here, when they threaten God's man again, God does not stay silent. Numbers 14:12: Adonai says, "I will strike them down with a plague and destroy them."

New Expectations

So what happened? Four times on the way *to* Mount Sinai the people complain and God hears their cries and delivers them. But three times on the way *from* Mount Sinai, in very similar circumstances of need and want in the wilderness, God does not put up with their behavior. God tells them to stop it.

What happened in between? God spoke the Torah. Before Mount Sinai they were runaway slaves, Egyptian property that had escaped. They did not know better, in other words. They had not yet seen the light. The light shone at Mount Sinai. It was the revelation of the word of God in the Torah. Now they were enlightened. Now they were equipped. Now they were made ready. Now they were strengthened. Now they were wise. Now they were God's own people.

When they continue on from there, and try the same behaviors they used before, God pushes back. The old story is no longer appropriate. The old behaviors are no longer acceptable. God will not put up with this runaway slave stuff any longer. God changes his strategy. God changes his calling and his expectations. God changes his will. The Torah makes that kind of a difference.

God Can Have New Thoughts

Let me conclude with three lessons we can take away from this difference in God after he has given the Torah from the way he was before he gave the Torah.

Lesson One

When the world changes God will sometimes change with it. God is not unable to adapt to changing circumstances on earth. God is free to act in new ways.

The other day I read an argument for the unchangeableness of God. It was the simple idea that since God is perfect he will not change because then he would be other than perfect. That is like saying Michelangelo's statue of David is a perfect human specimen and anything human that actually lives and grows and changes must then, necessarily, be less than perfect. A living God is greater than a static God with ideals of perfection. God is not less than alive and thinking and willing and doing.

His thoughts are great thoughts that can recognize how the free will of humanity is playing out and can recognize what tricks the Adversary is up to now. The Jews in the wilderness after they left Mount Sinai acted as if nothing had happened, as if nothing had changed in their time on that mountain. That was just not true.

There are times of God's revelation in your life, there are turning points in your life, in which God raises his expectations for you because you have changed, the world has changed and God is changing ahead of you. Sometimes God's plan changes with changing circumstances. He is wise that way.

Lesson Two

God's goals are always in the future, not in the past. God is forward looking. Keep in mind that God will build on the past. The Bible is a record of the triumphs of faith in the ancient past. God will build upon his word in scripture. But he is not building monuments for your life. There will be time enough for monuments to you when you are gone. Today, while it is day, God is at work changing people and changing times and changing nations in a way that is forward-looking, that is grounded in hope, that makes a difference for tomorrow.

He is telling the Israelites in the wilderness to let go of the past. Some of us need to hear that message. The focus has shifted from getting out of

Egypt to getting to the promised land. If someone is not able to make that paradigm shift and to begin thinking in the new ways that entrance into the promised land will demand then God is going to leave that man or woman behind. He actually discovers only two who can embrace the future: Joshua and Caleb. The rest do not fit any longer into God's plan. That is a terrible judgment. But they did it to themselves. They refused to change when God changed.

God brought his Torah into the world. That meant a new program. God was not going to sacrifice the success of his new program for sentimental reasons of carrying along ex-slaves who were victims in Egypt. God carried them so far. He carried them to the mountain, to the Torah. Then they had a real choice. God was on the move, and if only two people were going to move with him, then he would take the two. Better the two who were willing to adapt to change than the thousands who were not. Those are severe consequences, but it is a matter of free will.

What has God shown you about his plans for the future? What are your choices with regard to the will of God? Is God telling you he will no longer put up with your stuff? Maybe a new day is dawning for you.

God is on the Move

Lesson Three

Prepare for battle. God is not pushing back because the clock has run out. God is not pushing back because he has simply lost patience. God is not pushing back because he wants to us to be more religious, or more sacrificial, or more selfless. God pushes back because there is a war coming. It may be the promised land to them, but it is home to the Amalekites and the Hittites and the Jebusites, and God wants to change that. God has made a choice. He has chosen sides. He has chosen Moses and the Jews.

Some people still do not like that idea. Some people still do not believe that idea: that God will send his people to fight, to engage in battle, to win new territory. That is what he is doing with us. In these days God is raising up Messianic Judaism to take territory from Jews and from Christians. Much more than that we are on a mission to take territory away from Satan our adversary.

God is on our side. God is on the move. And he will not lose his fights because his soldiers are unprepared for battle. They left Egypt as runaways. They will arrive in Canaan as an army of conquest. What will change on the way? Observance of the Torah. Obedience to Torah. Living by Torah.

I confess I am not there yet. But I hear the clarion call. God is telling me to prepare for battle because he is on the move in our times. God knows I do not want to be left behind. The world is changing. God is changing. Messianic Judaism is one new step in his unfolding plan.

I am so grateful to belong to a God who will not sit idle, who will not give up, who is not done, who is not satisfied with the world as it is, but has goals for the future—goals that require human participation.

Let us not falter when God leads. Prepare yourself for battle. May God go with you in triumph and in conquest.

Discussion D: Judaism as Seen Through Christian Eyes

The Jews Have a Purpose of Their Own

In juxtaposition with Christianity, Judaism and Jewry will always lose. By Christian definition they are incomplete. Of course, it is Judaism that is to be compared with Christianity, not vice versa.

In 1983, Rabbi David Chernoff of Congregation Beth Yeshua in Philadelphia wrote *Yeshua the Messiah* as an introduction to Messianic Judaism. He begins chapter 1, "The Coming of the Messiah," with these sentences:

> For centuries, the ancient Jewish prophets foretold of One who was to come who would bring salvation and deliverance to God's Chosen People, Israel.
>
> In their extensive writings that spanned nearly two millennia, they gave clear prophetic "signposts" by which Israel could recognize the "Anointed One" and be prepared to receive Him when He came.[1]

This is a misleading premise. It either misrepresents the Jews as a people filled with empty messianic expectation for centuries or, if they ignored the signposts, it misrepresents God and the prophets as having a secret mission among the Jews for centuries on behalf of a future church to which they would not belong. The Jews did not exist nearly two thousand years for the purpose of delivering the messiah to the church.

---

1. Chernoff, *Yeshua the Messiah*, 7.

But that is a common narrative handed down from generation to generation in the church. Here is a formulation of it from the seventeenth century in the *Pensees* of the influential Christian thinker Blaise Pascal:

> The Jews had grown old in these earthly thoughts: that God loved their father Abraham, his flesh and what came forth from it; that because of this he had caused them to multiply and had distinguished them from all other peoples without suffering them to intermingle; that when they were languishing in Egypt he brought them out, with many great signs of his favour towards them; that he fed them with manna in the desert; that he led them into a very rich land; that he gave them kings and a well-built temple in which to offer beasts and be purified by the shedding of their blood; that finally he was to send them the Messiah to make them masters over the whole world and that he had foretold the time of his coming.
>
> When the world had grown old in these carnal errors, Jesus Christ came at the time appointed, but not in the expected blaze of glory, and thus they did not think it was he.[2]

It is a Christian perception that Yeshua came "in the fullness of time" (Gal 4:4) so that all the time leading up to his appearance was so much anticipation, preparation, and symbolism. It degrades the Jewish experience to order it according to the appearance of Yeshua the Messiah. It degrades the Torah as a second-rate revelation of God. It degrades the rabbis of the Mishna and Talmud as being men who were untimely born and who simply held open a teaching role that Yeshua would eventually come to fill.

Judaism Today is Not Really So Messianic

If Messianic Jews want to take their place at the table alongside Christians and Jews, we must get our history right. Yes, there were strong messianic expectations in the first century in some branches of Judaism, such as the Essenes, a group that organized itself in communities set apart from Jewish society. But they came and went over a short period, and no Jews since the first century have been related to the Essenes. Yes, there were messianic prophecies among the written prophets, but they were neither orderly nor extensive nor signposts giving direction. As Rabbi Michael Beals of Congregation Beth Shalom in Wilmington, Delaware once remarked to me, "The book of Isaiah does not mean as much to Jews as it does to Christians."[3] The

---

2. Pascal, *Pensees*, 111.
3. Personal conversation with the author.

party in Judaism to emerge as mainstream from the crucible of persecution during the period of the Second Temple (prior to 70 AD) was rabbinic and tannaitic. It diligently studied the Torah.

In my limited experience with Orthodox, Conservative, Reformed, and Reconstructionist rabbis and congregations, the only Jews I have seen spend time and energy waiting for a messiah were the Orthodox. Is Judaism a Messianic religion? If you address the question to the founder of the religion, Moshe, he will say it is not. Certainly religious victims of persecution—such as the Maccabean Jews of Alexander the Great's empire or the European Jews of the Middle Ages—hoped for deliverance from God. But the notion of Jewish incompleteness is a Christian myth created to enhance the Christian religious option by contrasting it with something less. Messianic Jews such as David Chernoff fall for it. He writes of Messianic Jews in the first century:

> They did not feel less Jewish by following Yeshua, but even more Jewish.
> They viewed their acceptance of Yeshua was a completion of their Judaism. They were completed and fulfilled as Jews because they had found the Messiah, and had found the Atonement which God had provided for them through this Jewish Messiah.[4]

Of course there are no verses from the New Testament or evidence from any other historical document to support the idea, "They did not feel less Jewish by following Yeshua, but even more Jewish," because the writer asserts it from his experience. It is a twentieth-century invention related to the church's ancient misrepresentation of Judaism as an inferior religion.

Inconvenient Options

Read Isaiah 45:1–8.

This is the oracle concerning Cyrus, the Persian ruler who defeated the armies of Babylonia in war and subjugated the country. One of his initiatives was to free the Jewish slaves. The prophet saw the hand of God at work in this turn of events. He imagines the Lord speaking to Cyrus "his anointed" or Cyrus "his messiah." Here is evidence that the messianic expectation that did exist in ancient Israel was not exclusive. It was not limited to one hope for one man of God for just one time. There are many "anointed ones" in

---

4 Chernoff, *Yeshua the Messiah*, 81.

the Hebrew Bible, including high priests and kings. Multiple anointed ones was an inconvenient truth for Christians reading through the scriptures for evidence to support their exclusive faith in Yeshua as the Anointed One.

All this matters not only because it is the biblical and historical truth but because it saves Messianic Judaism from the error of the myths of the completed Jew and the true Israel. We do not have to denigrate Judaism as an inferior religion in order to exalt Yeshua as messiah, as Lord, as king, as a son of God, as our blessed redeemer, as our merciful savior. Messianic Jews are neither the true Israel nor the true church. We are, instead, simply the true Messianic Jews.

Questions

1. Name some examples of juxtaposition in advertising (the model with the new automobile), in politics (the president before the Congress and Supreme Court justices, with invited guests, at the State of the Union speech), or in other types of persuasion or comedy (Abbot and Costello; Laurel and Hardy). Setting two things side-by-side can be defining. How did the church define itself this way in relation to Judaism?

2. Now Messianic Judaism is juxtaposed with both Christianity and Judaism. How do we look?

3. Some Messianic Jews see themselves as the true Israel, as the heirs to the promises God once gave to Judaism. Some Messianic Jews see themselves as the true church, as the body of Messiah who rightly understand Yeshua, who rightly follow the way, the truth, and the life he intended for his followers. How do you see your congregation in relation to Israel and in relation to the church?

10

Different Assumptions: Different Religion

Critics of Messianic Judaism say it is really a kind of Christianity dressed up in Jewish language and customs. Few observers take the opposite tack and say it is really a kind of Judaism using Christian beliefs and ideas. But what if Messianic Judaism is its own religion, drawing upon Christian and Jewish sources to create a different faith? What follows is a Messianic Jewish critique of Christian sermons, taking the approach used in chapter 6 for reading the book of Romans. The point is to examine the differences I see from my Messianic perspective. I bring a new set of assumptions to receiving God's word.

The battle for the establishment of a third biblical religion is won or lost in the assumptions, which are often unstated. The church helped establish itself apart from Judaism by changing the day of the Christian Sabbath. How? They assumed it.

An Idea Whose Time Had Come for the Church

Jews and Messianic Jews celebrate the Sabbath on the seventh day of the week while early on Christians began worshipping on the first day of the week. The reason for the shift and its timetable were not documented. Gentile Christians may have initiated the change in a positive desire to distinguish themselves from Judaism. Or, Jewish leaders may have banned

Christians from their Saturday services, prompting a defensive response of Sunday worship gatherings for Christians.

Regarding the worship schedule for the early church Laurie Guy observes:

> Originally on the Jewish sabbath, it quickly shifted to Sunday (the first day of the week). Hints of this shift appear in the New Testament itself and find confirmation in early second-century church history data.[1]

Guy cites Acts 20:7 and 1 Cor 16:2 as perhaps the earliest indicators. Then he quotes Bishop Ignatius of Antioch (35–108 AD) telling the Magnesians that to keep the Jewish tradition of the Sabbath rather than observing the Lord's Day on Sunday would be to "deny that we have received grace."[2]

There is no record of a debate. Other controversies were written about. This one was not. It probably was not disputed. Changes in assumptions can go down easily that way. Agreement and assent are given to a new idea, and almost immediately, people adjust. Former assumptions are hardly worth recalling because they are irrelevant.

The New Testament carries with it a grand set of assumptions. Twenty-seven books were chosen by the church because they basically share the same suppositions: suppose Christ is divine, suppose sin is original, suppose a new covenant is exclusive, and so forth. It is possible to suppose differently. Mary and Jesus, Zechariah and John the Baptist, Gabriel and Satan are all New Testament characters who appear in the Qur'an with a different set of assumptions. Mormons in the Church of Jesus Christ of Latter-day Saints suppose a different authority for the New Testament than its founders supposed. But Jews, on the other hand, did not bring their assumptions to the New Testament. They do not because Jews have never wanted to read it.

The majority of Messianic Jews recognize this alienation the same way the evangelical church does and do not expect Jews to come to the truth of the New Testament any differently than every non-believer. But Messianic Jews in the minority suppose that is not right. We suppose that a Jew who chooses to read the New Testament will do so with his or her own grand set of assumptions, which basically comes down to a monotheistic hermeneutic.

---

1. Guy, *Introducing Early Christianity*, 211–12.
2. Guy, *Introducing Early Christianity*, 40.

Different Assumptions: Different Religion 133

Fruits and Vegetables

This is taking up the New Testament in a new way. We reject the label of heretics because we refuse to belong to the church. Messianic Judaism should not be judged by the standards of Christian orthodoxy, just as fruits should not be judged by the standards of vegetables. They may look alike, children have to be taught the difference, and they have a lot in common in the supermarket. But they are not the same. Messianic Jews in the minority, whose views I am voicing in this exercise, likewise are not the same as Christians. Different assumptions have produced a different religion.

A Via Negativa: By Contrast

I am primarily interested in the assumptions of Messianic Judaism in co-opting the New Testament for its own religion. But rather than examine teachings by Messianic rabbis, I have instead assembled excerpts of New Testament sermons by Christian preachers with which I respectfully disagree as a Messianic Jew on the basis of their assumptions. Instead of a comparison, I am offering a contrast.

Bruce W. Thielemann, "When Mystery and Love Flow Mingled Down," First Presbyterian Church, Pittsburgh, Pennsylvania, Lent, 1989

> What do you think happened on Calvary? I'm not talking about the events, the people, the politics, the procedures of execution: I'm not talking about those things. And please, please don't give me some glib slogan. I'm not looking here for some theology that can be summed on a bumper sticker. You say to some people, "What happened on Calvary?" And they say, "Jesus died for our sins." What does that mean? How is it that one man can die for another? Why do sins have to be died for at all? Did God die? And how did what happened two thousand years ago have influence and impact on what's happening here today? You see that question, "What do you think happened on Calvary?" is a very profound question. The greatest theologians of the last two thousand years have wrestled with it and have presented profound theories of the atonement. And none of these has been able to encompass all the mystery of what occurred there. And

I certainly cannot encompass it this morning or in any other lifetime that might be mine.[3]

For Messianic Jews "all the mystery of what occurred there" is not as much as it is for Christians. The covenanting that God was doing on Calvary was not the covenant to displace all covenants. It was one more covenant in a string of them, going back to Abraham and including Noah and Moses and David. The assumption of ultimacy fits Jesus Christ as fully human and fully God. It does not fit the man of God through whom God is at work in a human sacrifice of atonement for sin. At least not in the same way.

From a Christian point of view, it is profound because it expands salvation beyond one people with one book and one language and one tradition and one set of covenants. Up until the Christ event, God had revealed himself to the Jews. In the Christ event, God revealed himself to the world. Jesus died for the sins of the world. Calvary was both Jewish history, and a new start in world history.

Not as much for Messianic Jews because God's relationship with the world had always existed through the Jews. In that sense, the Christ event was not a new act of God. The crucifixion of Christ was in line with the way God had been operating in the world all along—through the Jews. Yeshua is a Jewish messiah. If the rest of the world gets blessed by what God is doing with the messiah of the Jews that is to be expected. It has been promised all along as part of God's covenants with the Jews.

Karl Barth, "Look Up to Him!" Prison of Basel, Ascension Day, 1956

> But to look up to him, to Jesus Christ—his is our help! He is over us. He is in the centre of that encompassing mystery. He is in heaven. Who is Jesus Christ? He is the man in whom God has not only expressed his love, not only painted it on the wall, but put it to work. He is the principal actor who has taken upon himself and has overcome our human affliction, the injustice done by ourselves and by everybody else, our guilt and anxiety, our fate, even our death. These evils no longer threaten us from above. They are below us, even under our feet. He is the Son of God, who was made man in our likeness, who became our brother, in order that we may be with him children of the Father, that we may all be reunited with God and may share in his blessings: in his severe kindness and in his kind severity, and lastly in the eternal life for which we are meant and which is meant

---

3. Thielemann, "When Mystery and Love Flow."

> for us. This Jesus Christ, this mighty man, this Son of God is in heaven. And so is God. In the face of the Son the face of the heavenly Father is made to shine.[4]

We find here an instance of muddled thinking: "He is the Son of God, who was made man in our likeness, who became our brother." He sounds like an alien, and in the strictest sense that is what the Incarnation is. He is divine and fully God when you want him to be, and he is our brother and fully human when you want him to be. The assumption is you can have it both ways. Messianic Jews and Messianic Gentiles in the minority decide instead between the two ways of understanding Yeshua. Our assumption is that he was the man of God, a son of God by adoption, but only fully human. Like all the prophets before him, like all the kings of the Jews before him, like all the messiahs before him, he was born, not begotten.

Messianic believers do not observe Advent, Christmas, Epiphany, Lent, Holy Week, Maundy Thursday, Good Friday, Easter, or Pentecost. The reason we do not add the New Testament holidays on top of the Jewish holidays is that we are not initially endowed with salvation and redemption by Christ. We have it already through Abraham and Moses and David and the Torah and the Prophets and the Writings. Messianic Jews cannot be adopted by their heavenly father because that relationship is their birthright. Messianic Jews do not need to be "reunited with God."

There is another case of muddled thinking: the assumption "that we may all be reunited with God" means that even the Jews needed Jesus to die for them. Why? Because . . . Jews were not united with God. Really? When did that happen? When was the Old Testament voided? If it is enforced, Jews are not in need of Christ's salvation, redemption and new life are they? God did not reject the Jews and the Jews did not reject God. But some Christian thinkers assume as much. Messianic Jews must not.

Karl Barth, "Death—But Life!" Prison of Basel, Easter Sunday, 1959

> What is *death*, the wages paid by sin? Here again we must think beyond the first caption that may come to mind when we hear the word "death." Not only shall we die one day, Death is much greater and much more dangerous than that. It is the great "no," the shadow that hangs over our human life and accompanies all its movements. It is the judgment which reads: "You, your life or what you think is life has not meaning because it has no right to

---

4. Barth, "Look Up To Him!", 45.

> exist and therefore cannot last! Your life is a rejected life! It has no value before God or before your fellow-being, not even before yourself!" Death means that this "no" has been pronounced over us. Death means that we inescapably wither and wilt, returning to dust and ashes. This is death as paid by sin. This "no," this judgment, is the sum total of our paypacket. When we shall die at the appointed hour, the truth will be disclosed: the wages of sin is death.
>
> This is truly *our* history. One might also say that the history of the world is but one great demonstration of the fact that the wages of sin is death.[5]

Jews or Messianic Jews may read this and say, "Not us. Speak for yourself, goy. 'The shadow that hangs over our human life . . . the judgment' is not for us. We were born into God's family. Our life is not a rejected life. God promises he will never reject us."

My Baptist friends are thinking: "Nice religion." Nice and easy. Then I would remind them of Torah observance and ask them to compare their religious requirements. Then they would start quoting Paul, trying to nullify Jewish salvation because they work too hard at it. Finally we agree that we are talking about different religions. Exactly! With different assumptions. And God hears everyone's prayers.

Here is an instance of the assumption of the Christian doctrine of original sin. "This is truly *our* history" because the sin of Adam has become universal over the passage of time. Universal guilt requires a universal salvation. So Christ did not die just for some souls. It is no wonder that the Jews were offended by Paul's preaching. It insisted they change their assumptions and become part of a new religion.

Gardner C. Taylor, "A Strange Question in a Cemetery," NBC Radio, April 5, 1970

> Mary's love for her Lord posted her there in the hopelessness of the cemetery. That same stubborn, touching love put tears of great sorrow in her eyes and an immeasurable sadness in her heart. She had come to that human border where there was nothing to do but weep, and then came the strange question, so very strange to be asked in a cemetery, "Woman, why weepest thou?" Why ask such a question in a cemetery? A cemetery is a place for crying, for it writes *finis* over our love affairs. It is

---

5. Barth, "Death—But Life!", 147.

the scene of our earthly separations. A cemetery is a silent place where friends speak back to us no longer. It is a cold place where love's springtime is chilled in an unmalting winter. Why ask anybody, "Why do you cry" when that person is in a cemetery? What else is there to do? An inept, cruel question, unless it is Jesus speaking.

Faith declares that question to be not so strange on the first Easter morning, for Jesus was there in the cemetery and alive and said to her, "Mary," and his voice rang joyously in the saddened depths of her soul. It made a difference. Jesus was there and alive, and this made that cemetery so very different. It still does. I am sure we will go on weeping when we lose our loved ones, but we shall weep now as those who have hope. Jesus has been here now, and we can raise up our bowed-down heads. Jesus has been here now, and we can believe that while we may be separated we shall meet again where the load has lifted and the gate opens wide. Jesus has been here now, and we can believe that "life is ever lord of death, and love can never lose on its own." Jesus has been here now, and we can believe that somewhere there is a land beyond the river, a land whose fields are living green. Then let the glad anthems of Easter ring, for Jesus has been here.[6]

Matthew 17:1–8, Mark 9:1–8, Luke 9:28–36, and 2 Peter 1:16–18 tell of Jesus being glorified in front of three disciples. The three gospel accounts say that Elijah and Moses then appeared talking to Jesus. Luke adds the detail that they also appeared in glory. This account is the basis for an important Messianic distinction in regard to the meaning of Yeshua's resurrection from the dead on the third day.

For Paul and other New Testament writers the resurrection of Jesus Christ was a new act of God. Jesus was the first to be raised:

> But in fact Christ has been raised from the dead, the first fruits of those who have died. For since death came through a human being, the resurrection of the dead has also come through a human being; for as all die in Adam, so all will be made alive in Christ. But each in his own order: Christ the first fruits, then at his coming those who belong to Christ. (1 Cor 15:20–23)

My observation is that in his vision on the road to Damascus, Saul saw Jesus and heaven. Jesus was alone. Therefore Saul believed Jesus Christ could be the only way to heaven because Jesus was the only one to be raised

---

6. Taylor, "A Strange Question," 150–51.

from the dead. He surmised that resurrection was a new act of God begun with Jesus and upon which all other resurrections depend. It follows that because Jesus has been raised the rest of us may be also. This is the assumption behind the hope for reunion in heaven: "Jesus has been here now, and we can raise up our bowed-down heads."

This exclusiveness is problematic for Messianic Jews who do not believe that Jesus is the only way to heaven, nor is he the only one in heaven. God acted in Yeshua in continuity with his work with Jews. This is one thrust of the appearances of Moses and Elijah on the Mount of Transfiguration. They were already raised from the dead, before Jesus, before Easter. They were not simply visions without reality and they were not mythical or symbolic. They can be understood to signify the resurrection and glorification of the entire Jewish community, the entire nation of Israel, of which Yeshua was a part.

The difference Messianic Jews must insist upon is of Jesus revealing the resurrection of the dead—a different idea. Until Jesus appeared we did not know about rising from the grave. It was a revelation. It revealed something that went on as far back as Moses, at least. The apostle Paul would have agreed if he had seen on the road to Damascus what Peter, James, and John saw on the holy mountain. But he only saw Jesus and from that assumption we have Christianity.

Barbara Brown Taylor, "He Who Fills All in All," Ascension Day

> In a recent interview in *Common Boundary* magazine, novelist Reynolds Price talked about why he, a devoted Christian, does not go to church. Part of it, he says, is disillusionment dating from the civil rights era, when the white southern Christian church, he says, "behaved about as badly as possible." But that is not the only reason.
>
> "The few times I've gone to church in recent years," he says, "I'm immediately asked if I'll coach the Little League team or give a talk on Wednesday night or come to the men's bell-ringing class on Sunday afternoon. Church has become a full-service entertainment facility. It ought to be the place where God lives."
>
> And yet, according to Saint Paul, it still is. The roof may be gone, and there may be sheep grazing in the nave, but Christ is still there—half a face, with one wide eye looking right at us, one hand raised in endless benediction—still giving his blessing to a ruined church. He cannot, or will not, be separated from his body. What God has joined together, let no one put asunder.

> Say what you will about the arrogance of supposing that Christ needs the church as much as the church needs Christ. Paul says that we are his consummation, the fullness of him who fills all in all. Without us, his fullness is not full. Without him, we are as good as dead. He may not need us, but he is bound to us in love. We are his elect, Paul says, the executors of God's will for the redemption of the cosmos.[7]

The church is the Body of Christ. It is both spiritual and physical, both mystical and actual, bringing together the glorified Christ in heaven with the members of his church on earth. By the spirit of Christ they experience his presence and power in their hearts and lives. Messianic Jews do not pursue or conceive of this experience. While we also experience spiritual fulfillment and exaltation, for Messianic Jews only God is omniscient. Not even in resurrection does Yeshua have divine consciousness.

The closest thing to an intermediary between God and humanity in Judaism is the preexistent Torah. This is both spiritual and physical, both mystical and actual, both heavenly and earthly. But it is not divine, God himself. Like Wisdom, it is a manifestation of God. Wisdom is also personified and exalted to a divine level. For Messianic Jews, Yeshua is the personification of the Torah but he does not share its preexistence.

Not incidentally, perhaps, before God gave the church its mission, he bestowed upon the Jews their election and mission to bless all the families of the earth.

Austin Farrer, "Christ is God," Trinity College Chapel, Oxford

> The evidence accompanying his earthly life is his miracles. Spiritual men have at all times done wonderful things; if Christ had not done any it would have surprised us. His divine nature is not proved by his miracles, but it is confirmed by them. . . .
>
> The evidence succeeding his earthly life is his resurrection. His friends were convinced by it immediately, and turned into a believing church by it. His enemies never claimed that they possessed or could exhibit his body. The resurrection sealed the Father's acceptance of the Son's supreme sacrifice.
>
> Last of all we may put what we will call retrospective evidence. When the disciples came to look back and ask how the divine Saviour had come into the world, the answer was, By a divine and virginal birth. Faith will accept this retrospective

---

7. Taylor, "He Who Fills All," 138.

evidence as in agreement with what faith already believes, and as something divinely appropriate; but the virginal birth cannot convince unbelief, for how are we to produce the witnesses?

It is almost absurd to count over the heads of evidence at this rate. It is more like a catalogue than a sermon, and it would be quite useless if I were not reminding you of things you know already. I will make just one point now, and it shall be something quite general. It is this: all of this evidence is addressed to faith, and to nothing but faith.[8]

Miracle workers before Yeshua—6: Moses, Joshua, Samson, Elijah, Elisha, and Daniel.

Resurrections before Yeshua—3: The son of the widow of Zarepheth, the son of the Shunamnite woman, and the man raised out of Elisha's grave.

Men born to women called barren whose births were attributed to supernatural intervention before Yeshua—8: Isaac, Esau, Jacob, Joseph, Benjamin, Samson, Samuel, and John the Baptist.

Ascensions before Yeshua—2: Enoch and Elijah.

The Messianic Jewish agenda is not to tear down the Christian faith. The point in citing these other lives from the Bible is to create a juxtaposition with the life of Yeshua which shows him to be the man of God and messiah of Israel we know him to be. He is a character like other biblical characters, with his own revelation, mission, and greatness. It is a life and story in continuity with the history of Israel. It connects with the miracles, it connects with the resurrections, it connects with the miraculous births, it even connects with the ascensions. It also connects with the Torah, with the covenantal tradition, with the election and with the salvation.

The miracle of the virgin birth is a Christian article of faith. It is thought to have conveyed sinlessness since sin is imputed to us through the sex act. That is a Christology that Messianic Jews can live without in order to believe in Jesus without being polytheistic. For the Messianic minority he was bone of our bone and flesh of our flesh and a better person than we are—maybe the best who ever lived. We get it wrong; he got it right. So we follow him. We are not trying to be Christians. Instead we would be Torah-observant Messianic Jews and Gentiles.

---

8. Farrer, "Christ is God," 35–36.

11

The Bible Without Old and New Testaments

The appearance of Messianic Judaism is an offense to traditionalists who rely on established ways of relating to God and reading the Bible. Messianic believers break through the boundaries of orthodoxy set around Jesus and the New Testament as well as break the taboo against Jewish connection to Jesus. We are inclusive where Christians and Jews are exclusive. We bring a new light to bear on interpreting scripture.

But a monotheistic faith in Jesus is not that odd since it developed historically at the same time Christian orthodoxy was establishing itself. It is odd that it has taken so long to revive. Related to the establishment of the church is the pejorative name of "Old Testament" they gave to the Hebrew scriptures. Maybe there is a better light to shine on that boundary marker.

Who Is the Bible For?

Basic Bible Interpretation by Roy B. Zuck is a valuable contribution to the diverse field of biblical hermeneutics. It offers its own set of correct answers using, among other things, axioms and corollaries.

"Axiom One" is that the Bible is a human book. The second corollary from that is, "Each biblical writing was written by someone to specific hearers or readers in a specific historical, geographical situation for a specific purpose."[1] Professor Zuck conveys this idea with an image from everyday life:

> Suppose you go to someone's house and you see a note on the door with the words, "Come in and wait." At first you may be tempted to go in, but then you ask yourself, Was this written to me? If not, who is the note for, and what problem or situation is being addressed by the note?[2]

Different Assumptions

Let us say this note is the book of Genesis or the book of Psalms or the book of Micah. It was written for the Jews. After all, it is in Hebrew. Who else could it be for? Years later the Christians come calling and assume it is for them. They knew there must be a note somewhere so they went looking for it at the house where Jesus lived.

It all sounds reasonable. But then, having apprehended the note—Genesis, Psalms, Micah, and the rest—the Christians asserted that it was only for them. The original claim of the Jews was supplanted. Jewish writings were now the old covenant that had been superceded and were properly understood only as a companion to the new covenant—the New Testament. Not surprisingly, the Jews rejected this new companion and held on to the historical reality that the note on the door had been written for them.

Both Christianity and Judaism are exclusive with regard to the Bible. Messianic Judaism, by contrast, is inclusive. We find the note on the door, in Hebrew, at the house where Jesus lived, and we are happy to have both Christians and Jews, as well as ourselves, be addressed by it. For Christians and Jews, this happiness is suspicious.

Messianic Jews Adopt the Christian Method

A problem for many people is the exclusive texts in the Bible, some on the Jewish side and some on the Christian side. Our Messianic Jewish solution is to adopt the whole Bible for our religion and explain away the difficult passages that contradict our beliefs. Christian exegetes have shown us how this is done. Christians either just ignore the Bible verses that give exclusive promises to the Jews (Gen 17) and safeguard their covenants (Deut

---

1. Zuck, *Basic Bible Interpretation*, 64.
2. Zuck, *Basic Bible Interpretation*, 64.

28) or reinterpret them in an act of robbery and carry them into their own storehouse.

Common methods of reinterpretation are typology, allegory, prophetic reading, and dispensationalism. But they involve work. It is easier just to assume the Bible is addressed to you as a Christian and everything in it is material for the Holy Spirit to speak through. Unspoken, unexamined assumptions make the exegetical leap easy. You just assume.

Messianic Jews get it from both sides, however. Very few, if any, Jews rise up to challenge the church's re-use of their Hebrew scriptures. I imagine centuries ago some tried, but they were so quickly put to death that the protest just ceased. Messianic believers are in the position of having to explain to Jews our allegiance to the New Testament and having to explain to Christians our allegiance to the Torah, the Prophets, and the Writings. To make it easier on ourselves we often concede to Christians the idea of the Bible with its Old Testament. But we should not.

A Messianic Jewish solution for explaining away the difficult passages in the New Testament that contradict our Jewish beliefs is akin to the church's practice of ignoring or reinterpreting exclusive Hebrew texts. When Paul writes in a way that eradicates Jewish identity, we have to decline to participate. For example, in the Letter to the Ephesians, wanting to exalt Christ over all, Paul reconciles the Gentiles in his audience with Israel:

> For he is our peace; in his flesh he has made both groups into one and has broken down the dividing wall, that is, the hostility between us. He has abolished the law with its commandments and ordinances, that he might create in himself one new humanity in place of the two, thus making peace. (2:14–15 NRSV)

Being rid of the Jews is a logical extension of abolishing their commandments, and this "one new humanity" is an impossible abstraction. Messianic Jews can pass on it.

When Paul writes to his church about "the Jews, who killed the Lord Jesus and the prophets and also drove us out . . . In this way they always heap up their sins to the limit. The wrath of God has come upon them at last" (1 Thess 2:15–16), we just ignore the parts about, well, everything after "the Jews."

The Necessity of Reinterpreting Scripture

Mostly though we reinterpret away difficulties. When John writes in his gospel, "In the beginning was the Word, and the Word was with God, and the

Word was God. He was with God in the beginning. Through him all things were made; without him nothing was made that has been made. In him was life, and that life was the light of all mankind" (John 1:1–4), we can interpret this to mean that Jesus was an incarnation of the Torah. These are things Jews believe about the Torah.

Christians of course have a different doctrine of incarnation, with "the" in front of it and a capital "I." They also have doctrines of the Trinity (same grand punctuation) and the sacraments that are not part of Messianic Judaism. These teachings of the church inform their hermeneutics and exegesis.

The way of Messianic reinterpretation is not that elaborate. It is based on the idea that the act of God in Messiah Yeshua was not unique, but in keeping with the other acts of God revealed in the Hebrew scriptures. Sarah's post-menopausal conception of Isaac was as miraculous as Mary's virginal conception of Jesus. A virgin birth does not have to convey divinity any more than a post-menopausal miracle.

A Human Messiah

Jesus said, "Anyone who has seen me has seen the Father. How can you say, 'Show us the Father'? Don't you believe that I am in the Father, and that the Father is in me? The words I say to you I do not speak on my own authority. Rather, it is the Father, living in me, who is doing his work. Believe me when I say that I am in the Father and the Father is in me'" (John 14:9–11). To us these sound like the words Moses spoke to Pharaoh. God was in Moses and, perhaps, in a sense, Moses was in God. It depends on the meaning of "in." We can make it work. Recall Moses going into God:

> When Moses entered the tent of meeting to speak with the LORD, he heard the voice speaking to him from between the two cherubim above the atonement cover on the ark of the covenant law. In this way the LORD spoke to him. (Num 7:89)

Like Moses, Jesus was a chosen one, and like Moses, he established his own covenant with God.

A Case Study

An early Christian hymn is quoted by Paul in Philippians 2:6–11. It expresses the truth of the Christian religion. Messianic Jews are not Christians, and yet we bind ourselves to these words of the New Testament. We must reinterpret them for our own religion and faith:

> Who, though he was in the form of God,
> did not regard equality with God
> as something to be exploited,
> but emptied himself,
> taking the form of a slave,
> being born in human likeness.
> and being found in human form,
> he humbled himself
> and became obedient to the point of death—
> even death on a cross.
> Therefore God also highly exalted him
> and gave him the name
> that is above every name,
> so that at the name of Jesus
> every knee should bend,
> in heaven and on earth and under the earth
> and every tongue should confess
> that Jesus Christ is Lord,
> to the glory of God the Father. (NRSV)

For a Jew to conceive of this, she has to draw distinctions that a Christian would not make. For a Jew, it is significant and essential that he was merely in the form of God and was not God. The distinction at the start is that God is by himself—picture him—and the one in the form of God is someone else, a separate being, a different face. Being in the same room, on the same platform, beside one another if you will—that is equality.

Another obstacle is in the phrase "being born in human likeness." The key is to put the stress on the word "born." Jesus was born. That means, whatever words you use to qualify it, that he was a man, a human being, a member of the human race. He was born—like Moses, Joshua, Samson, Samuel, David and all the rest. The next line, "being found in human form," is really not difficult to understand as a saying or euphemism.

The ending sounds a bit familiar to us when we recall Isaiah 60:3, "Nations will come to your light, and kings to the brightness of your dawn." The confusion in English Bibles of "Lord" in the New Testament with "LORD" in the Old Testament is not a big deal for Christians, but of course it is essential for Jews. The name in all caps was someone's idea of conveying a non-word with letters. But it only works in reading. It utterly fails in hearing. All distinctions are lost.

Can a Messianic Jew believe that Yeshua is Lord? If he was the incarnation of the Torah, he should be. The Torah rules. Messianic Jews, more than anyone, want to believe that the whole world will come under its authority.

This was not the apostle Paul's idea, nor is it the Pope's, nor is it the rabbis', but once a text is let loose into the world it is open for anyone's interpretation.

An Historical Precedent from the First and Second Centuries

What Messianic Jews have in their favor in relation to the New Testament is history. In the first and second centuries AD, the early years of the church, there were also Jewish, Torah-observant followers of Jesus. They lost in a competition with the proto-orthodox church to inherit Jesus's mantle of authority. Nevertheless outside the apostles' successful church establishment there existed for many years these early believers who looked something like Messianic Jews. They left few traces but were organized enough to have a name and make some enemies. They were called Ebionites. Professor Bart Ehrman profiles them in his book on textual criticism because early New Testament texts sometime give evidence of their determination to believe in Jesus with a monotheistic faith. He writes,

> We know of a number of Christian groups from the second and third centuries that had an "adoptionistic" view of Christ. This view is called adoptionistic because its adherents maintained that Jesus was not divine but a full flesh-and-blood human being whom God had "adopted" to be his son, usually at his baptism.
>
> One of the best-known early Christian groups who held to an adoptionistic Christology was a sect of Jewish-Christians known as the Ebionites. We aren't sure why they were given this name. It may have originated as a self-designation based on the Hebrew term *Ebyon*, which means "poor." These followers of Jesus may have imitated the original band of Jesus's disciples in giving up everything because of their faith, and so taking upon themselves voluntary poverty for the sake of others.
>
> Wherever their name came from, the views of this group are clearly reported in our early records, principally written by their enemies who saw them as heretics. These followers of Jesus were, like him, Jews; where they differed from other Christians was in their insistence that to follow Jesus one *had* to be a Jew. For men, this meant becoming circumcised. For men and women, it meant following the Jewish law given by Moses, including kosher food laws and the observance of Sabbath and Jewish festivals.
>
> In particular, it was their understanding of Jesus as the Jewish messiah that set these Christians apart from others. For

since they were strict monotheists—believing that only One could be God—they insisted that Jesus was not himself divine, but was a human being no different in "nature" from the rest of us. He was born from the sexual union of his parents, Joseph and Mary, born like everyone else (his mother was not a virgin), and reared, then, in a Jewish home. What made Jesus different from all others was that he was more righteous in following the Jewish law; and because of his great righteousness God adopted him to be his son at his baptism, when a voice came from heaven announcing that he was God's son.[3]

Messianic Judaism may be a kind of reemergence of this defeated faction of Jesus followers. Still separated from orthodox Pauline Christianity, we must now reinvent ourselves as another religion, a third biblical religion. We lost our scriptures. We are stuck using the church's New Testament because we cannot exist without the sacred stories and divine revelation from the first century—the evidence of Jesus's appearing and our only historic link to him. We have to make do with Christian writings to go along with the traditional Jewish scriptures that also instruct us. Adaptation is our divine calling.

Dropping the "Old Testament"

A piece of this adaptation is renouncing the Christian term "Old Testament." "New Testament" might work in a chronological sense: the Greek writing of the apostles of Jesus is the newest covenant or testament in the series of covenants God has made through the ages. But labeling the earlier covenants "old" was meant to be pejorative and by our lights is erroneous.

At Princeton Theological Seminary's Institute of Theology in 1970, James A. Sanders put forward a proposal for the church to abandon the division of old and new testaments. He based his argument on the historical record. A Messianic Jewish reinvention of the Bible's classifications would correspond to the facts in a similar fashion. Professor Sanders lectured on the "Significance & Authority of Canon":

> You understand that the Old Testament is proto-Christian. The Old Testament is proto-Christian. It's also proto-Jewish but that's their problem. You must not read Judaism back into the Old Testament. This is a great fallacy, particularly in the popular mind: the Old Testament is Jewish and the New Testament is Christian. That's not really right. The New Testament is Jewish. The Old Testament is a mixture of old Israelite material and of

3. Ehrman, *Misquoting Jesus*, 155–56.

early Judaism in the writings and in the editorial work on the Law and the Prophets.

The simple breakdown that the Old Testament is Jewish and the New Testament is Christian doesn't make any sense at all. One thing you can be very sure of, however else you describe the Old Testament, the New Testament is Jewish. It comes from one of the two denominations that survived the destruction of the Second Temple. There were only two that did survive out of early Judaism: that is Pharisaism and Christianity. And the Pharisees become rabbinic Judaism and Christianity moves on toward the western world and more deeply into the northeast from that point.

I want to change—I want to set—some attitudes, if I may, and that's one. The other is that we might divide the Bible not into the Old and New Testaments at all, in order to get away from the old vision, but to divide it in the following manner: to speak of the Law and the Prophets, on the one hand, and the Writings, gospels and epistles on the other hand.

The Law and the Prophets on the one hand and the Writings—that is to say the third section of the Old Testament, you remember from seminary training. This is the poetical materials, Psalms, Proverbs, Job and so on and so forth—the five scrolls and the rest—and the gospels and epistles.

The reason being, I want to make this following thesis: the Bible comes to us out of ashes of two temples. The Bible comes to us out of the ashes, the destruction, of two temples. That which we call the Law and the Prophets was formed out of those materials of ancient Israel which survived the destruction of the northern and southern kingdoms. That is to say, which survived the destruction of the old nationalist cults of Israel and Judah.

We often speak now of how we inherit only perhaps ten percent of the literature from that period. There was an attitude in certain textbooks some years back that what we have in the Bible is what they had and the only question is to talk about how it got together. But we don't talk that way anymore. On the contrary, we know that what we have in the Law and the Prophets was filtered through the experience of the crucifixion, filtered through the experience of the destruction of the institutions—political, cultic, social and cultural—of ancient Israel.[4]

---

4. Sanders, "Significance & Authority of Canon."

The First Century Texts

His reorganizational plan was the starting point for an hour-long lecture, and Professor Sanders did not return to it with any more detail. He groups the Law and Prophets by themselves because they alone reach back in time before the destruction of the First Temple. He groups the Writings and the gospels and the epistles because (a) they share a time frame dominated by the destruction of the Second Temple, and (b) they are all Jewish writings circulating in Israel at that time. This actually works for Messianic Judaism.

12

Renewed Fear

Torah Lesson: Exodus 18:1–20:23
Beit HaTorah
February 11, 2012

Introduction

We are all familiar with the New Testament. But how about the Renewed Testament of the Messianic Jews? They are both the same and different. To join Messianic Judaism, I had to stop being a Christian—sometimes more in theory than in practice. But I have not left too soon, which is the cautionary tale of Jethro the Midianite who converted to serving the God of Israel only to depart before God issued the requirements. He didn't get his future. I have still got mine. I am afraid to miss it.

What a Miracle Looks Like

Do you have in your memory bank an image of something that everyone else in the world has forgotten, but it stuck with you, and you have never been able to forget it? It seemed random at the time—it was random. But somehow you remember. The random became personal. That is what a miracle in the Bible can look like when God goes after someone. He makes the random personal. That is what he was doing that day on the mountain. There is nothing as random as an earthquake—unless a prophet told you three days before, "Be ready for the third day." Then the earthquake was on purpose. The thunder and lightning were on purpose. The thick cloud was on purpose.

The Fear of Him Upon You

So the people were afraid. The nation of Israel was afraid. Then what does the prophet say? "Do not be afraid." If he hadn't said anything three days ago they might have thought they were just having peculiar weather. They are afraid now because of him! They are trembling because of him. Now he wants them to quit it, to give up their fear—the fear he started! Chapter 20, verse 20 declares: "Moses said to the people, 'Do not be afraid; for God has come only to test you and to put the fear of him upon you so that you do not sin.'"

This is called a paradox. Two opposite things are both true at the same time: do not be afraid *and* be afraid. Don't be afraid of being afraid. Do not fear fear itself. This is a good fear: so do not be afraid of it.

You want to fear God. That is the appropriate response to meeting God: being afraid. Trembling. Letting go of your grip on all those secure things that keep you being who you are where you are. You are now in the presence of God. Shake. It will be good for you. Not to shake, not to tremble, not to fear in the presence of God—that is not so good. The thing is: how many of us really fear God today? Fear God so that we do not sin?

Maybe this message is not for you, but you will not mind overhearing it a bit while I might talk to someone who is not afraid to disregard God. That is what Moshe is talking about when he says our being afraid of God is to keep us from sinning. Give God regard. Give God our thoughts and concerns and priority.

Our Own Way of Doing Things

Some people are not afraid to not pray. Some people are not afraid to not read the Bible. Some people are not afraid to not keep the Torah. Some people are not afraid to not give money to the poor, to the needy, to the orphan. Some people are not afraid to not visit people in prison or in nursing homes or who are shut in. Some people are not afraid to not tithe, to not keep the Sabbath holy, to not live a holy life.

Some people are just not afraid of God. They do not fear walking away from his word, from his directions, from his will, from his hope, from his plan and purpose. You know that. Some people live their lives as though it is all up to them. Then they wonder why they are not happy or fulfilled or content.

God has told you what is good, O man. And what does man do? Decides for himself what is good. Disregards God. Not fearing the consequences.

I work everyday with men who have learned to fear. It is a joy for me to see them reclaiming their lives from drug and alcohol addiction. They are generally the happiest they have ever been because they learned to fear doing things their own way, they learned to fear the consequences of addiction, they learned to fear taking that first drink or that first drug because they know it will lead to them to having no where to go, to sleeping out in the streets or in the woods, to losing their jobs and family and everything that they count as dear in their lives. It does not mean they actually tremble at the thought of picking up and using. But they respect the power of the disease, the power of the drug. They fear it. So they go to AA and NA meetings. They get a sponsor to help them stay clean and sober. They work the twelve steps. They work hard at recovery because they fear relapse.

We ought to fear relapse as well, relapsing into our own ways of doing things—relapsing from our devotion to God, our sacrifice for God, our obedience to God, our care for God and our thoughts for God; relapsing back to a time and place where we did not love God as we know we should, as we know we can. As we know we must. Let us fear a relapse to when we did not have fear in our relationship with God.

The Father-in-law

I want to spend a little time talking about Jethro, the priest of Midian, who was Moshe's father-in-law. He is the man who missed the Ten Commandments, who missed the giving of the law. He is like the disciple Thomas who was away when Jesus made his resurrection appearance to his disciples. Thomas missed the glory of Yeshua in the resurrection. Jethro missed the glory of Adonai in the commandments.

But Thomas came back. We never hear of Jethro coming back. He returned to Midian before learning how to keep the Torah, how to observe God's commandments, how to walk in God's ways. So what do you suppose happened? Most likely he relapsed back into his old Midianite way of doing things. Because he didn't know what he didn't know. He knew God. He knew the Lord. He knew HaShem. But he didn't know HaShem enough to fear him.

Of course you can choose your friends, but you cannot choose your family. Moshe married into Jethro's family. His daughter brings home Moses one day and says, "Daddy, this is the man I want to marry." Jethro says, "Zipporah, there are plenty of nice Midianite boys. Why don't you find someone of your own tribe? These mixed marriages never work out." Zipporah sticks to her guns: "But Daddy, I *love* him." So Zipporah and Moses get married, and pretty soon Moses is leading a slave revolt in Egypt and leading the people of Israel out across the desert. Jethro's son-in-law is a hero—a big shot. He faced down the Pharaoh and won. What fellow in Midian could say that? His son-in-law is famous. So Jethro goes out in the desert to see him after Zipporah and the kids visited for a while.

That first night they are sitting around the fire, and Moshe tells him everything that happened down in Egypt and how the God of Israel really took it to Pharaoh and the Egyptians. Jethro was really happy. He was proud of Moses. The scriptures say he rejoiced: "Jethro rejoiced for all the good that the LORD had done to Israel, in delivering them from the Egyptians (Exod 18:9 NRSV).

What happens next? What happens next is that Jethro, the Midianite priest to the Midianite gods—a priest to other gods—blessed Adonai. He proclaimed, "Blessed be the LORD, who has delivered you from the Egyptians and from Pharaoh" (18:10 NRSV). Jethro blessed Adonai, and he made sacrifice to the God of Israel. He became a convert. He converted from polytheism to monotheism.

"Now I know that the LORD is greater than all other gods," he tells everyone (18:11). That is what he knows. He knows HaShem is all alone above all his gods. He has no other god before Adonai. He makes a sacrifice: probably a bull or a heifer because he fed a number of people afterwards.

It was a great day. Moshe had succeeded in bringing his pagan father-in-law, a priest in another religion, into a saving relationship with the God of Israel. The Gentile becomes a Jew. The Arab becomes one of the children of Israel.

A New Opportunity

Until he is not. Until the children of Israel receive their inheritance and their birthright: the law of God to determine how to be Israel, how to be in covenant with God, how to fear the Lord. By the time that day comes, Jethro has already left, none the wiser. He was headed back to Midian.

Look at the contrast in chapter 19 to what went on with Jethro in chapter 18. In Exodus 19:4, we have HaShem's version of what happened down in Egypt. Just like Moshe was telling his father-in-law the story, here God is giving his own words to Moshe to retell it to the people down below: "You yourselves have seen what I did to Egypt, and how I carried you on eagles' wings and brought you to myself."

God can tell stories too. Just as Moshe told the story of the Exodus in a way that persuaded his father-in-law, so God is telling the same story in different words in order to persuade a different audience: the people of Israel.

After the story, verse 5 begins in my New American Standard Bible translation with "Now then." Have you ever been addressed that way? Maybe it was by your parents or a teacher or a boss. He or she begins by telling a story. You begin to get into the story and enjoy the moment and suddenly there is this shift, this shift in attitude, this shift in expectation: "Now then."

"Now then, we are going to talk about you." Now then, the agenda has shifted—and you are now who we are talking about. "Now then. . . ." Pause.

"Now then . . ." Something is coming. The other shoe is about to drop. "Now then. . . . *if*." Your ears pick up at that. "If." If what? Here it comes.

> "Now then, if you will indeed obey My voice and keep My covenant, then you shall be My own possession among all the peoples, for all the earth is Mine; and you shall be to Me a kingdom of priests and a holy nation" (Exod 19:5–6 NASB).

That priest from Midian left too soon. Now Adonai, the God of Israel, is talking about a priesthood of his own. Moses is going to lead a kingdom of priests. But Jethro will not be among them. It turned out the story was only the first part.

Getting the story and blessing the Lord and making sacrifice was all preliminary to what was really on God's heart and mind: how to create the future. The past was prelude to the future. The rescue from Egypt was only the first part. An important part, certainly. Never forget it. But it is incomplete without "Now then. . . ."

Building a Future

Now then, there are ramifications. Now then, there is work to do. Now then, there is a new identity to adopt. Now then, there is a new way of seeing things, a new way of doing things.

"Now then. . . ." Is God building a future with you? Has there come a point in your worship of God, in your relationship with God, in your walk with him, that the Lord speaks to you with "Now then . . . ?"

Worship is good, prayer is good, relating is good—but it is all for a purpose. It is all for a reason. What is that purpose for you? Why does God have your attention? What is the reason you are here? What is the reason you serve the God of Israel? What is your future with God?

Jethro never heard it. Jethro never got it. This Arab Gentile did not really become a Jew, did he? No. He left before the revealing of the Ten Commandments, before the giving of the law, before the giving of the identity as a kingdom of priests and a holy nation. He didn't get a future. He walks off and is never heard from again. After a couple more generations the Midianites are extinct—never heard from again.

The Jews, on the other hand, become a great people: a holy nation. Holy means "set apart." Israel began to fear that third day. That was when they were set apart, made holy. They were made God's own possession among all the peoples of the earth. They were given a future.

On Our Own

When we begin to fear God enough to keep his commandments, we discover ourselves to be the Messianic believers. Because Messianic Judaism is to become a part of the future that God is giving to the Jews and to Israel.

If you want to know God through Torah observance you cannot be a Christian. That is what Messianic Jews have discovered. It just does not work. It does not work to have the sacraments of baptism and Holy Communion, to follow a calendar year that begins with Advent, followed by the seasons of Christmas and Epiphany and Lent and Easter and Pentecost, if you are Torah observant. If you are Torah observant you keep other holidays.

If you have the Torah, you do not need the Apostles' Creed or the Nicene Creed or the Westminster Confession to tell you what to believe. If you have the Torah you do not belong to a denomination of the Christian church. There is no pope or bishop or conference or General Assembly to follow.

So we are set apart from Christianity—and from Judaism. Jews will deny a messiah has come and Christians will deny the permanence of the Torah. Many Christians—and some Messianic Jews as well—now deny the permanence of God's promises to Israel. Such people think God is ready to give up, or already has given up, on the Jews and transferred his promises to them—either these certain Christians or these certain Messianic Jews. They foolishly calculate it to be so.

If It Were Easy More People Would Be Doing It

So we are out there on our own. But God's truth was never established in the world by a popular vote. God Almighty has never won an election at a state university, never won a vote in the media. The Torah has never won a popularity contest in America. The Torah and Messiah Yeshua together—well, they get even fewer votes together than they do apart.

What we have in Messianic Judaism that is unique but true is the Renewed Covenant. We use that name in our liturgy every week when we read from the New Testament: the *Brit Chadeshah*. You may think it a small matter, or you may not have given it much thought at all, but it defines Messianic Judaism apart from Christianity and apart from Judaism. It means, on the one hand, that we have a covenant with God that Judaism does not have, does not acknowledge, does not believe is possible. It means, on the other hand, that we have a renewed covenant with God that is different from the new covenant in Christianity. The church does not acknowledge this possibility. The church does not agree that for some people the grace of God comes as a renewal. For them there is only a new covenant—the New Testament.

It is the same books, the same Yeshua the messiah—Jesus the Christ—the same birth, the same life, the same teaching, the same arrest, the same trial, the same beatings, the same tree to hang on, the same crucifixion, the same last words, the same death and—glory to God—the same resurrection from the dead. It is the same covenant of grace for Christians and for Messianic Jews. We are saved by grace through faith.

But for Messianic Jews it is not a new covenant of election—as Paul and other Greek writers talk about it. For Messianic Jews it is a renewed covenant of grace for people who are already elected through God's choice of the Jews in Abraham, God's choice of the Jews in the Torah of Moses, God's choice of the Jews in David, God's choice of the Jews in the promise of the land of Zion to the Jews. We have atonement and salvation through the death of Yeshua, but not election. We have atonement and salvation through the death of Yeshua as a renewed covenant. We are saved by a messiah as people already chosen by and in relation to God on a prior basis. We are Messianic.

Both the Same and Different

Now how can the same thing, the same set of words, the same covenant agreement, mean different things to different people and both be true? How can we come to the church and ask for its New Testament and rename it and reapply it and take it away from the sacraments and the church calendar and the church history and the church creeds and confessions and say it is now true for us differently: as a renewed covenant?

We can because it is God's truth. We can because it is not true for us as a new covenant, but it is as a renewed covenant.

You can think of it in terms of the way we understand people. All of you know me as the son of Bill and Kathleen Dandoy. Being their son is a truth of my life. But there is someone else who knows me as her husband. It is also an historical fact that I have been married to Lesley for thirty years. Both relationships are true about me. But in one I am a son and in the other I am a husband. I am also, in addition, a father to two people. That is just as true as my being a son and being a husband. Someone's parent, someone else's child, someone else's spouse—I am the same man with three different titles based on three different relationships.

Or think of it in terms on an event. To some people it was the War Between the States, to others it was the Civil War. There is a distinction. It was the same event, the same battles, the same losses, the same destruction. But Lincoln and the North insisted that the nation was divided—a civil war—while Lee and Jefferson Davis and the states of the Confederacy experienced it as some states separating from other states and being prevented from doing so by the invasion of northern troops. They invoked the same Constitution, but one side read it as an agreement between states and the other side read it as the charter of a nation. Different assumptions were both true at the same time.

Or think of it in terms of a story, like one of Jesus's parables. Parables can have more than one meaning, more than one application, more than one truth. Yeshua taught us this.

A Case Study

Take for example the parable of The Dishonest Steward at the beginning of the sixteenth chapter of the gospel of Luke (16:1–13). The steward learns he is going to be let go and is not going to get any severance pay or unemployment checks. So he goes and gets a list of his master's creditors, finds out what they owe, and goes to each of them and cuts a deal. He will do them a favor and when he is turned out maybe they will remember his favor and take him in. One owes a hundred measures of oil. He tells him, "Take your bill, and sit down quickly and write fifty" (16:6 RSV). That will cover it. He does this with the wheat account as well. The parable ends with a twist: "The master commended the dishonest steward for his prudence" (16:8 RSV).

That is the parable. A difficult one, isn't it? So Luke helps us out by giving not two or three interpretations of it, but four. Get the parable this way:

> "[F]or the sons of this world are wiser in their own generation than the sons of light." (16:8 RSV)

Or this way:

> "And I tell you, make friends for yourselves by means of unrighteous mammon, so that when it fails they may receive you into the eternal habitations." (16:9 RSV)

Or this way, as a parable of judgment:

> "And if you have not been faithful in that which is another's, who will give you that which is your own?" (16:12 RSV)

Or, finally, in Luke 16:13:

> "No servant can serve two masters: for either he will hate the one and love the other; or he will be devoted to the one and despise the other. You cannot serve God and mammon." (RSV)

Now which one of the four is the true meaning of the parable? Which one did Jesus have in mind? Well, Luke puts all four interpretations in the quotation marks of Jesus. Jesus probably said all four, given different audiences and different occasions and different lessons. So there was one parable, one set of words, one story—that was true in different ways.

A True Story

This is the audacious and true claim of Messianic Judaism. We are that person who is known differently in different relationships. We are that event that is understood differently by different groups of people. We are that story that is true in a different way but is just as true nevertheless.

We are the children of the renewed covenant. Judaism has its covenants that are true and everlasting. Christianity has its new covenant that is true and everlasting. We do not find ourselves belonging to either religion. Instead, we belong to Yeshua and we belong to HaShem in ways that neither the Christians belong to Jesus nor the Jews belong to Adonai. We are people who, in our own generation, have heard the voice of God. That voice has said to each of us in our own time and place: "Now then. . . ."

Renewed Fear 159

"Now then...." God says: "What about your future? What about my agenda? I am doing a new thing in Messianic Judaism. I am setting people apart in a new way: as a holy nation, as a kingdom of priests. Made holy by the blood of the Lamb. Made priests by Yeshua the High Priest." We are a people with a past—with a past election. We are people with a future—with a future grace.

Our response here, individually and collectively, has been to fear HaShem: to fear the Lord—for we are in the presence of God. We are afraid not to obey. We are afraid not to listen. We are afraid not to be Messianic. We cannot deny the covenants and the promises of Israel. We cannot deny the messiah and savior of Christianity. If we do either we are lost—for sure.

So here we stand. We can do no other, so help us God. Amen.

Conclusion

The format of the nightly service at the 2018 MJAA (Messianic Jewish Alliance of America) conference did not change for the concluding Shabbat. Along with praise and worship and an offering, there were three teachers. Rabbi Jeff Forman of the City of David congregation in Toronto was the final speaker, and he began with some Canadian humor before quickly moving into a message that was going to challenge the assembly. He set up the decision he would offer with a prophetic word directed to him at another conference.

I Hear the Lord Saying

In the telling of it he mixes his voice with the voice of the minister who was given this prophecy by the Holy Spirit, so there is overlap between the bishop and the rabbi. With Jeff Forman's permission, here is a transcript from the middle portion of this rabbi's teaching that night:

> Recently, I attended a pastors' conference in the Toronto area in Canada, and I prayed over someone, and the speaker, his name is Bishop Tony Miller, maybe some of you know him, he's an interesting guy. But before he started speaking one night, he said, Where's that rabbi? And he stood me up in the midst of about 800 people and he released a prophetic word that was not just for me. It is for our movement. And I believe it's right in line with what we heard earlier in the week, that the vision, what we're hearing all week long. He said, I heard the Lord say when you were praying tonight that there's an assignment that's coming on to your life—and again I was representing our movement to him, I believe—according to Acts 15 to reestablish the fallen booth of David. And that while many would be seeking

to restore ceremonial realities, there's a grace that's going to be on your life—and on this Alliance—to bring them to a living presence. That's what we're about. And when that happens, and I don't know what you do, he said, but I hear the Lord saying there is a reestablishment of the kingdom in a way that David saw it. And the key of David is going to be extended through you—through us. And the Gentiles will come running to it. And there's a strong wind that's blowing in your favor. I believe that.

And I don't know what this means for you in particular but I hear the Lord saying you're not going to be on the side street any longer. It's time to go Main Street. Hallelujah. The Nicodemus anointing that's been there, that you have come by night to get the information you needed—God's about to remove you from the side street to the Main Street because the kingdom of David and the throne of David are being restored in this generation. The days are at hand and the fulfillment of every vision. Hallelujah. God says I'm going to put this side street stuff to rest, this idea that our movement is on the fringe of the Jewish community. No, its time to go Main Street. That is a strategic shift. That's like the shift that took place in the days of David, in the days of the sons of Issachar, you know this verse, who understood the times and knew what Israel should do. And what did they understand? That it was time to turn the kingdom of Saul over to David. Friends, the days are at hand and the fulfillment of our Messianic vision. The religious or the spiritual kingdom is shifting from the stronghold that rabbinic Judaism has had on our people. And there's a strong wind blowing in favor. And we are looking upon him whom we have pierced and mourning as one mourns for an only child, as we restore the Jewish face of Yeshua and the Jewishness of this gospel. The Holy Spirit is unlocking Jewish hearts and opening Jewish eyes.[1]

Stuck on the Side Streets

In the context of a vision for growth with greater success and influence in the world is an acknowledgment that, after four or five decades as a movement, Messianic Judaism is stuck on the side streets of religious life in America, Israel, and elsewhere. David Chernoff observes, "But it was only after 1967, when Jerusalem was back in Jewish hands, that the modern movement of

---

1. Forman, et al., "Erev Shabbat."

Messianic Judaism really came into being."[2] Paul Liberman dates it to the July 1975 national conference of the Hebrew Christian Alliance of America which approved a name change to Messianic Jewish Alliance of America. That was a passing of the guard.[3] Depending on the reckoning, therefore, Bishop Tony Miller's prophetic word in 2018 was either fifty-one or forty-three years into the modern movement.

That is the span of a generation, and at the 2018 MJAA conference, recognition was given to a rising generation of leadership for the movement. There are certainly signs of vitality in Messianic congregations and associations as well as in the faith of individuals. New congregations continue to form and new converts continue to join. Messianic Jewish books continue to find their audience. In 2018, Kathie Lee Gifford came out with a Messianic title, *The Rock, the Road, and the Rabbi*, that made bestseller lists. New music is being produced, and new artists are recording.

A Vision of the Future

Rabbi Jeff Forman, part of the movement's founding generation, received the prophetic word as truthful and fit it into his own understanding of the challenges and limitations with which the Messianic movement struggles. But he did not go on to describe his vision of life on Main Street. Perhaps it is as a renewal movement in Judaism. Perhaps it is as a renewal movement in the church.

Or perhaps it is neither in Judaism nor in the church that the future of the Messianic movement will unfold. Perhaps it will find its place in the Main Street of society as a third biblical religion. That is the burden of these pages.

In Tension with the Mainstream

In 1985, Rachel L. E. Kohn made a study of "Hebrew Christianity and Messianic Judaism on the Church-Sect Continuum." Acknowledging the limits of her research, she then draws the conclusion that Messianic Judaism is a sect of the church ("placed at the sectarian end of the church-sect continuum").[4] Further on she discusses it in terms of the assimilation of these Jews into

---

2. Chernoff, *Yeshua the Messiah*, 77.
3. Liberman and Wasson, *Don't Call Me Christian*, 224.
4. Kohn, "Hebrew Christianity and Messianic Judaism," 180.

the pluralistic "majority community" of America, as though it is a sect of Judaism as well.[5]

She uses a sociological paradigm for the church-sect continuum with "three aspects of sub-cultural deviance" that can create tension in relationship to the larger community: "difference, antagonism and separation."[6] Low degrees of tension in these areas would be signs of belonging and assimilation. High degrees of tension in difference, antagonism, and separation would be signs of sectarianism and factionalism: side street.

Jeanne Nigro, a popular lecturer, speaks of addressing her Christian audience and her Messianic audience.[7] It is an easy distinction to recognize and fits Kohn's judgment that Messianic Judaism is somewhere on a continuum in its relationship to the church that puts it in tension with the mainstream. The Messianic movement began as an alternative to joining the church, defining itself as an outsider to the established church.[8] Of course a continuum with Judaism exists as well and the tension there is even more exacerbated.[9] Evangelical Messianic Jewish writers generally assume that non-Messianic Jews are unsaved and unenlightened.[10]

5. Kohn, "Hebrew Christianity and Messianic Judaism," 185–86.
6. Kohn, "Hebrew Christianity and Messianic Judaism," 10.
7. Nigro, "God's Strategic Plan."
8. Liberman recalls the question at the creation of the movement: "Yet, for almost two thousand years, Jews have been expected to drop their Jewish identities, blend into churches, and to effectively become Gentiles to accept the Jewish Messiah. This is not right, and we must reverse it and take a stand against this idea! If the Gentiles did not have to become Jews, should the Jews have to become Gentiles?" Liberman, *Don't Call Me Christian*, 219.
9. Harris-Shapiro recognizes the conflict, "In order to explain this anomaly, Messianic Judaism, almost since the group's inception, has been labeled a cult by the mainstream Jewish community, on the assumption that adherents have to be brainwashed into their assertion that one could believe in Jesus and remain Jewish." Harris-Shapiro, *Messianic Judaism*, 2. And, "Messianic Judaism challenges the normative Jewish community to articulate its own boundaries. A seemingly simple task on the surface, it proves surprisingly difficult." Harris-Shapiro, *Messianic Judaism*, 168.
10. David Chernoff addresses Jews with the gospel, "In fact, if Yeshua truly is the Jewish Messiah, then all Jewish people everywhere should accept Him without delay! There is only one way to find out. We all have to go back to the Word of God ourselves, study the Messianic prophecies and find out the truth about this man of Galilee. . . . Yeshua claimed to be the Messiah. He claimed to be the Son of the living God." Chernoff, *Yeshua the Messiah*, 82–83. Sam Nadler teaches a replacement theology, "Since the Mosaic *torah* fulfills its purpose in showing us our great need for mercy and grace in Yeshua, it results in condemnation if we seek salvation and glory from it. That the glory upon the face of Moses was fading demonstrated the limited glory that could come from the Mosaic *torah*. The New Covenant is thus 'a ministry of righteousness,' since we receive God's righteousness in Messiah. The glory that the Spirit gives through the New Covenant far surpasses the glory derived from the Mosaic *torah* (2 Corinthians 3:4–6).

Messianic Jews Do Not Fit In

These contrasts and conflicts are not at the heart of Messianic Judaism. They are not necessary to it. Carl Kinbar observes,

> All forms of Messianic Judaism have at least these three characteristics in common: they embrace the unique status of the person, words, and work of Yeshua the Messiah; they view the Scriptures as normative; and they observe some level of traditional Jewish practice.[11]

He goes on to say that "the status of Yeshua and the Scriptures is normative" while congregations differ in their emphasis of tradition. The majority of Messianic Jews hold to the high Christology of evangelical Protestantism as well as a high view of the inspiration of scripture. Ironically, for Messianic Jews, that is life at the margins. For Jewish Christians who have converted and assimilated into the church, it is not. They fit in. But Messianic Jews do not fit in—not into the church nor into Judaism. We are a religion unto ourselves.

In 2013, Messianic Rabbi Mark Kinzer pondered "the twenty-first-century evolution of the movement." He was inspired that, "A vocal minority has called for radical identification with the Jewish community and an identity distinct from the evangelical world."[12] The paradigm shift that will set Messianic Judaism free with a distinct identity will be trusting in a new soteriology, a new ground of salvation, that is true to its roots in Christianity and Judaism and true to its new revelation.

The Way Forward . . .

We are a religion unto ourselves when we reject trinitarianism and high Christology for Jewish monotheism. As Joseph Shulam observed in an earlier quotation, "Anyone who wants to make Yeshua into God has lost his way on his journey of faith."[13] The way forward out of sectarianism and into the mainstream of society is for Messianic Judaism to take the radical step of reading the New Testament as a testimony to the man Yeshua and his

---

The Mosaic *torah* was the promise; the New Covenant *torah* was the fulfillment of the promise. The lasting glory of the Mosaic *torah* is Yeshua Himself. All of its other glory was to fade away, to be nullified, whereas Messiah and His glory is to remain forever." Nadler, *Messianic Foundations*, 197–98.

11. Kinbar, "Messianic Jews," 72.
12. Kinzer, "Messianic Jews," 134.
13. Schneider, "Messianic Jews Debate," 21.

experience of God. Fifty years ago Messianic Jews took the radical step of breaking from Judaism. It is time for the movement to break from evangelicalism. There is more power and influence and salvation waiting in a future that finds its way to a low Christology, a liberal view of scripture, and an open-minded embrace of the legitimacy of traditional, Talmudic Judaism.

. . . With the Living God

Karl Barth could be critical of the church for not relating to God on God's terms. In that mood he held up this mirror:

> To a greater or lesser extent, the Church is a vigorous and extensive attempt to humanize the divine, to bring it within the sphere of the world of time and things, and to make it a practical 'something', for the benefit of those who cannot live with the Living God, and yet cannot live without God (the Grand Inquisitor!).[14]

This might sound like what a low Christology and liberal view of scripture and open-mindedness to other faiths will establish: "a vigorous and extensive attempt to humanize the divine." That would be failure. But low Christology leads to high theology. That God was with this man Yeshua and together they did all that—even a new covenant with atonement for sin—is a message of truth and reconciliation the world needs and may be waiting for.

Messianic Jews can live with the living God. We are his idea. It is a call for taking another way home: a way we walk on our own, not by the lights of the Jewish faith and not by the lights of the Christian faith. It is a fearful thing to fall into the hands of the living God. He is our Fear and our salvation.

---

14. Barth, *Epistle to the Romans*, 332.

Bibliography

Bainton, Roland H. *Here I Stand: A Life of Martin Luther*. Nashville: Abingdon, 2013.
Barth, Karl. "Death—But Life!" In *Deliverance to the Captives*, translated by Marguerite Wieser, 144–51. New York: Harper & Row, 1961.
———. *The Epistle to the Romans*. 6th ed. Translated by Edwyn C. Hoskyns. New York: Oxford University Press, 1968.
———. "Look Up to Him!" In *Deliverance to the Captives*, translated by Marguerite Wieser, 43–50. New York: Harper & Row, 1961.
———. "The Strange New World Within the Bible." In *The Word of God and the Word of Man*, translated by Douglas Horton, 28–50. Gloucester: Peter Smith, 1978.
Beker, J. Christiaan. *Paul's Apocalyptic Gospel: The Coming Triumph of God*. Philadelphia: Fortress, 1982.
Bell, Richard H., ed. *Seeds of the Spirit: Wisdom of the Twentieth Century*. Louisville: Westminster John Knox, 1995.
Brunner, Emil. *Our Faith*. Translated by John W. Rilling. New York: Charles Scribner's Sons, 1954.
Buzzard, Anthony F., and Charles F. Hunting. *The Doctrine of the Trinity: Christianity's Self-inflicted Wound*. San Francisco: International Scholars, 1998.
Calvin, John. "Calvin's Commentaries: Acts 18." Bible Hub. Accessed March 10, 2013. https://biblehub.com/commentaries/calvin/acts/18.htm.
———. "Christ's Titles." In *A Calvin Reader*, edited by William F. Keesecker, 42–43. Philadelphia: Westminster, 1985.
Chernoff, David. *Yeshua the Messiah*. Havertown: Kesher Ministries International, 1983.
Earhardt, Ainsley. *The Light Within Me*. New York: HarperCollins, 2018.
Ehrman, Bart D. "Did Jesus Think He was God?" Lecture #7 in *How Jesus Became God*. The Great Courses, online video, 2017. https://www.thegreatcourses.com/courses/how-jesus-became-god.
———. *Misquoting Jesus: The Story Behind Who Changed the Bible and Why*. New York: HarperSanFrancisco, 2005.
Farrer, Austin. "Christ is God." In *Austin Farrer: The Essential Sermons*, edited by Leslie Houlden, 33–36. Cambridge: Cowley, 1991.
———. "The Painter's Colours." In *Austin Farrer: The Essential Sermons*, edited by Leslie Houlden, 1–4. Cambridge: Cowley, 1991.
Fishbane, Michael. *Text and Texture*. New York: Schoken, 1979.

Bibliography

Forman, Watnik, et al. "Erev Shabbat." Messianic Jewish Alliance of America Conference. Messiah College, July 6, 2018. www.mannarecording.com.

Freedman, Harry. *The Talmud: A Biography*. New York: Bloomsbury, 2014.

Gill, John. "Introduction to Ezekiel 40." Bible Study Tools. Accessed on March 10, 2012. https://www.biblestudytools.com/commentaries/gills-exposition-of-the-bible/ezekiel-40-introduction.html.

Guy, Laurie. *Introducing Early Christianity: A Topical Survey of Its Life, Beliefs & Practices*. Downers Grove: InterVarsity, 2004.

Hashivenu. "Core Value #1: Messianic Judaism is a Judaism." Accessed April 25, 2020. http://hashivenu.org/core-value-1/.

Harris-Shapiro, Carol. *Messianic Judaism: A Rabbi's Journey through Religious Change in America*. Boston: Beacon, 1999.

Harvey, Richard. *Mapping Messianic Jewish Theology: A Constructive Approach*. Colorado Springs: Paternoster, 2009.

Heschel, Abraham Joshua. "Mission to the Jews." In *I Asked for Wonder: A Spiritual Anthology*, edited by Samuel H. Dresner, 110–11. New York: Crossroad, 1998.

———. "Prayer." In *Moral Grandeur and Spiritual Audacity: Essays*, edited by Susannah Heschel, 340–53. New York: The Noonday, 1996.

———. "To Be a Jew: What Is It?" In *Moral Grandeur and Spiritual Audacity: Essays*, edited by Susannah Heschel, 3–11. New York: The Noonday, 1996.

Hunt, Helen, dir. *Then She Found Me*. 2007. Chatsworth: Image Entertainment, 2007. DVD.

Jews for Judaism. "Meeting the Challenge: Hebrew Christians and the Jewish Community." July 28, 2020. https://jewsforjudaism.org/knowledge/articles/meeting-challenge-hebrew-christians-jewish-community/.

John Paul II. "To the Representatives of the Jewish Community." Translated by Agata Gliwa. Apostolic Journey to Poland. June 9, 1991. http://www.vatican.va/content/john-paul-ii/en/speeches/1991/august/documents/hf_jp-ii_spe_19910818_comunita-ebraica.html.

Juster, Daniel C. "Biblical Authority." In *Voices of Messianic Judaism*, edited by Dan Cohn-Sherbok, 19–27. Baltimore: Messianic Jewish, 2001.

Kinbar, Carl. "Messianic Jews and Jewish Tradition." In *Introduction to Messianic Judaism: Its Ecclesial Context and Biblical Foundations*, edited by David Rudolph and Joel Willitts, 72–81. Grand Rapids: Zondervan, 2013.

Kinzer, Mark. "Messianic Jews and the Jewish World." In *Introduction to Messianic Judaism: Its Ecclesial Context and Biblical Foundations*, edited by David Rudolph and Joel Willitts, 126–35. Grand Rapids: Zondervan, 2013.

Kohn, Rachel L. E. "Hebrew Christianity and Messianic Judaism on the Church-Sect Continuum." PhD diss., McMaster University, 1985.

Liberman, Paul, and Jack Wasson. *Don't Call Me Christian*. Arlington: Tishbite, 2015.

McKee, J. K. "Introducing the Divinity of Yeshua." Lecture handout. Messianic Jewish Alliance of America Conference: Messiah College, July 6, 2018.

Merton, Thomas. "Fire Watch, July 4, 1952." In *A Thomas Merton Reader*, edited by Thomas P. McDonnell, 210–23. New York: Image, 1989.

Moo, Douglas J. *Romans: The NIV Application Commentary: From Biblical Text to Contemporary Life*. Grand Rapids: Zondervan, 2009.

Nadler, Sam. *Messianic Foundations*. Columbia: Word of Messiah Ministries, 2010.

Niesel, Wilhelm. *The Theology of Calvin*. Translated by Harold Knight. Grand Rapids: Baker Book House, 1980.

Nigro, Jeanne. "God's Strategic Plan for the Future," Messianic Jewish Alliance of America Conference: Messiah College, July 3, 2018.

Office of the General Assembly Presbyterian Church (USA). "A Theological Understanding of the Relationship Between Christians and Jews." Louisville, 1987. https://www.pcusa.org/site_media/media/uploads/_resolutions/christians-jews.pdf.

Pascal, Blaise. *Pensees*. Translated by A. J. Krailsheimer. New York: Penguin, 1977.

Rausch, David A. *Messianic Judaism: Its History, Theology and Polity*. Lewiston: Edwin Mellen, 1982.

Roberts, F. Morgan. "A Friend for Every Time and Place." In *Are There Horses in Heaven? And Other Thoughts*, 89–93. Pittsburgh: Lighthouse Point, 1996.

Rosenzweig, Franz. "The Church and the Synagogue." In *Franz Rosenzweig: His Life and Thought*, edited by Nahum N. Glatzer, 341–43. New York: Schocken, 1961.

Rubin, Yitzchak. "What was G-d's purpose in creating man?" In *Fifty Days for Fifty Years: Remember the Past to Build the Future*, 90–91. London: The Union of Jewish Students, 1995.

Ruderman, David B. "On Studying Jewish History." In *Between Cross and Crescent: Jewish Civilization from Mohammed to Spinoza*. The Great Courses, DVD video, 2005.

Rudolph, David. "Messianic Judaism in Antiquity and in the Modern Era." In *Introduction to Messianic Judaism: Its Ecclesial Context and Biblical Foundations*, edited by David Rudolph and Joel Willitts, 21–36. Grand Rapids: Zondervan, 2013.

Sanders, James A. *God Has A Story Too: Sermons in Context*. Philadelphia: Fortress, 1979.

———. "Significance & Authority of Canon." Institute of Theology: Princeton Theological Seminary, July 1, 1970.

Schneider, Aviel. "Messianic Jews Debate the Deity of Jesus." *Israel Today*, November, 2001.

Steinberg, Milton. *Basic Judaism*. New York: Harcourt, Brace & World, 1947.

Stern, David H. *Restoring the Jewishness of the Gospel: A Message for Christians*. Clarksville: Messianic Jewish, 2009.

Taylor, Barbara Brown. "He Who Fills All in All." In *Home By Another Way*, 135–41. Cambridge: Cowley, 1999.

Taylor, Gardner C. "A Strange Question in a Cemetery." In *The Words of Gardner Taylor, Volume 1: NBC Radio Sermons, 1959–1970*, edited by Edward L. Taylor, 148–51. Valley Forge: Judson, 1999.

Tenenbom, Tuvia. *Catch the Jew!* New York: Gefen, 2015.

Thielemann, Bruce W. "When Mystery and Love Flow Mingled Down." Sermon. First Presbyterian Church: Pittsburgh, 1989.

Union of Messianic Jewish Congregations. "Defining Messianic Judaism." UMJC Theology Committee, July 20, 2005. https://www.umjc.org/defining-messianic-judaism.

Warren, Rick. *The Purpose-Driven Life Prayer Journal*. Grand Rapids: Zondervan, 2003.

Wex, Michael. *Born to Kvetch: Yiddish Language and Culture in All Its Moods*. New York: St. Martin's, 2005.

Wikipedia. "Messianic Judaism." *Wikipedia: The Free Encyclopedia.* Accessed April 29, 2020. https://en.wikipedia.org/wiki/Messianic_Judaism.

Willitts, Joel. "Conclusion." In *Introduction to Messianic Judaism: Its Ecclesial Context and Biblical Foundations,* edited by David Rudolph and Joel Willitts, 315–19. Grand Rapids: Zondervan, 2013.

Zionist Organization of America: Brooklyn Region. "Fighting for Israel and Winning." May 7, 2020. zoabrooklyn.org.

Zuck, Roy B. *Basic Bible Interpretation.* Colorado Springs: David C. Cook, 1991.

Index of Names

Barth, Karl, 6, 9, 134–35, 135–36, 165
Beals, Michael, 68, 128
Beit HaTorah congregation, 4, 5, 9, 13, 27, 28, 97, 101, 107, 110, 118, 150
Beker, J. Christiaan, 95–96
Biblical Literacy, 101
Brunner, Emil, 100, 102, 105
Buzzard, Anthony, 111–12

Calvin, John, 6, 11, 57–58, 104
Chernoff, David, 115, 115n, 127, 129, 161–62, 163n
Church of Jesus Christ of Latter-day Saints (Mormons), 28–29, 41, 113, 132
Congregation Beth Yeshua, 115, 127
Creeger, Sariella, 5, 9, 116
Cyrus of Persia, 6, 44, 129

Dallas Theological Seminary, 16, 17
David, 11, 58, 90, 91, 107, 135, 156, 160–61

Earhardt, Ainsely, 6
Ebionites, 146–47
Ehrman, Bart D., 7, 146–47
Ezekiel, 27, 32–33, 34, 36

Farrer, Austin, 19, 139–40
Fishbane, Michael, 25
Forman, Jeff, 10, 160, 162

Full Gospel Business Men's Fellowship, 55–56

Gifford, Kathie Lee, 162
Gill, John, 32
Guy, Laurie, 132

Haman the Agagite, 47
Harris-Shapiro, Carol, xviii, 1–2, 55, 163n
Harvey, Richard, xiv, xvn, xviii–xviiin, xvii, 14–15, 16, 18n
Hashivenu, 53–54
Hebrew Christian Alliance of America, see Messianic Jewish Alliance of America
Hebron, 42–43
Heschel, Abraham Joshua, 48–49, 58, 107–08
Hunt, Helen, 50

Ignatius of Antioch, 132
International Alliance of Messianic Congregations and Synagogues (IAMCS), 17
Israel Today, 15–16

Jehovah's Witnesses, 28–29, 113
Jethro, 150, 152–55
Jewish Community Relations Council of New York (JCRCNY), 51–53
Jews for Judaism, 51–53
John Paul II, Pope, 107, 109

Index of Names

Juster, Daniel, 17

Kinbar, Carl, 164
Kinzer, Mark, xiv, 164
Kohn, Rachel L.E., 162–63

Levinas, Emmanuel, 106–07, 109
Liberman, Paul, 51, 55, 162, 163n
Luther, Martin, 6, 9, 17, 61

McKee, J.K., xvn, xvin
Meeting Ground, 5, 102
Messianic Jewish Alliance of America (MJAA), 2, 4, 9, 10, 15, 18, 51, 55, 160, 162
Mikveh Yisrael congregation, 110
Miller, Tony, 10, 160–162
Moo, Douglas J., 61–62, 90
Moses (Moshe), 25–26, 40, 84–85, 87, 90–91, 100, 101, 115–16, 119–23, 125, 135, 137–38, 140, 144, 145, 146, 151–54, 163n–64n

Nadler, Sam, 18n, 163n–64n
New Calvary School of Ministry, 62
Niesel, Wilhelm, 11
Nigro, Jeanne, 163

Pascal, Blaise, 56, 128
Paul (Saul, Sha'ul), 17, 29, 30, 31, 33, 57, 58, 61–96, 100, 103–04, 105, 114, 116, 136, 137, 138–39, 143, 144, 146, 156
Potok, Chaim, 1
Presbyterian Church (USA) (PCUSA), 5, 6, 8, 10, 54

Princeton Theological Seminary, 6, 147

Rausch, David, 14–15
Romney, Mitt, 28–29
Rosh Pina congregation, 9
Rosenzweig, Franz, 106–07
Roth, Sid, 55
Rubin, Yitzchak, 49
Ruderman, David B., 38–39, 41

Sanders, James A., 118, 147–49
Shulam, Joseph, 15, 22, 164
Sneiderman, Eliezer, xviii
Steinberg, Milton, 45–46
Stendahl, Krister, 61–62
Stern, David H., 4n, 16, 19n

Taylor, Barbara Brown, 138–39
Taylor, Gardner C., 136–37
Tenenbom, Tuvia, 42–43
Thielemann, Bruce W., 133–34
Tzur, David Tel, 15–16, 22

Union of Messianic Jewish Congregations (UMJC), xvi, 15, 17, 18

Warren, Rick, 121
Wex, Michael, 39–40, 41
Willitts, Joel, 13, 17, 20, 22
World Council of Churches, 3, 54

Yisroel, Adam, 16, 22, 37, 110–12

Zionist Organization of America, 48
Zuck, Roy B., 17, 141–42

Index of Subjects

Another way home, 101–03, 165
Assumptions, 132, 157
    Christian and Jewish, xiii
    Christian, 23, 62, 109, 131–33, 135, 136, 138, 142–43
    Evangelical, 79, 109
    Jewish, 22–23, 49, 50, 62, 136
    MJ, xiii, 131, 133
    mistaken, 40, 95–96
Atonement, 4n, 7, 22, 44, 77, 91, 97–98, 99–100, 104, 156

Bible
    addressed to, 143
    as authority, xiii, 17, 117
    Biblical faith, 103, 107
    ours too, xviii, 23, 117, 142
    study of, 40, 62, 107

Christianity, 1, 127, 131
    as a branch of Judaism, 4n
    features, 3, 114
    rejected, 15, 114, 116, 117, 164
    relationship to Judaism, 106–07
Christians
    dialogue with Jews, xviii, 8, 54
    exclusivistic, 17–19, 30, 52, 63, 91, 107, 114, 138, 142
    heirs to the promise, 68, 142
    identity, 4n
Christology, 7–8, 117, 140, 165
    Christologies, 7, 95
    high Christology, 95, 116, 164

Messianic, xvn, 18n
Church, 67
    co-opt Hebrew scripture, 22, 25–26, 44, 142, 147
    foundation, xv
    heresy, xvii, 16, 23, 28, 45, 133, 146–47
    MJ branch of church, 37, 41, 162
    MJ sect of church, xiv, 24, 115, 162–63
    related to MJ, xv–xvi, 3, 9, 51, 156–57
    relations with Jews, 8, 38–39, 54, 104, 107
    supercedes Israel, 23, 30, 39, 54, 62, 67, 75, 76, 77, 83, 113, 115, 127–29, 143, 155
    traditions, 3, 114
    without Jewishness, 19n, 56, 163n
Church calendar, holidays, 3, 10, 23, 34, 114, 135, 155, 157
Conversion, 3, 4–6, 9–10, 28, 55, 78, 101–03, 153
Covenant, 8, 11, 77
    dual covenants 44, 93, 105, 106–08, 114, 116, 134
    God initiated, 56, 70, 83, 116, 120, 134, 138
    Jewish birthright, 53, 55, 79, 98–99, 104–05
    Mosaic, 25–26, 85, 87
    new and old, 9, 58, 114, 134, 159
    renewed covenant 58, 113, 156, 158

Index of Subjects

Double movement of faith, 58–59

Election, 8, 63, 66, 74–75, 98, 104, 159
  by Christ, 36, 138
  diversity in, 61
  of Israel, 68, 75, 84, 139
  prior to birth, 68–69
  sovereignty over all, 70
Eschatology, 3, 4, 22, 30, 34, 35, 45, 47, 88, 92, 95–96
Evangelical MJ, xv, 15, 18–19, 45, 108–09 114, 132, 163–64, 165
  background, 15, 55–56
  conservative, 18–19
  MJAA, 2, 4, 9, 10, 15, 55, 160–62
  UMJC, xvi, 15, 17

Fundamentalism 14–15, 17, 19, 56

God (Adonai, HaShem, LORD)
  of the Bible, xii, 10, 64, 111, 113
  blessing from, 4n, 12, 87, 134
  of both Christians and Jews, 8, 54, 66, 83, 107, 134, 142
  in covenant, 53, 83, 120, 134
  experience of, xiv, 1, 4–6, 56, 101–02
  as Father, 36, 66, 99, 105, 106, 144
  of the Jews, 8, 90, 121, 122–23, 125, 135
  means of grace, 58, 59, 61, 114
  mercy of, 22, 70, 74, 76, 93, 105
  MJ new idea of, xii, 19, 23, 26, 31, 37, 126, 165
  as one, xv, xvn, 15–16, 145
  progressive revelation, xii, 31, 124–25
  revealed, 10, 83–84, 99–100
  revealed in Jesus, 31, 66, 81, 114
  revealed in Jews, 4n, 121, 134
  revealed to Moses, 25–26, 85, 104, 120, 125, 144, 154
  saving act, 58, 137, 153
  as Son, 7, 66, 134–35, 144, 145
  soul formation, 48–50
  sovereignty, kingdom, 4, 70, 72, 89, 93, 120
  the Spirit of, 17
  of the Torah, 31, 101, 104, 122–26
  as Trinity, 7, 16, 111
  wrath of, 71, 72, 73, 75–76, 89, 123

Hermeneutic
  Christian, 20–22, 26, 44–45
  infallibility of Bible, 17
  Messianic, 22, 44, 45, 113, 116, 141, 142–44, 144–46
  Messianic paradigm, 20, 23, 117, 142
  monotheistic, xv, xviii, 132
  post-supersessionist, 20
  third way, xvi
Holy Spirit, 5, 17–18, 22, 161
  Baptism of the, 22, 55–56, 113
  Spirit-filled, 2, 10, 55–56, 160–61

Incarnation, 3, 52, 66, 116, 135
  as doctrine, xv, 18, 44, 144
  hypostatic, xv
  of Torah 144, 145

Jesus (Yeshua)
  as alien, xv, 135
  in Christ, 44, 58, 61, 63, 65, 68, 76, 105, 116
  as divine, xv, xvin, 16, 66, 135
  fully human, xv, 7, 23, 52, 54, 56, 110–12, 135, 140, 144–45, 164
  as living Torah, 29, 31, 116, 139, 144, 145
  as Lord, xviii, 65, 66, 79, 82, 91, 103, 106, 145
  a messiah, xv, 36, 43–44, 60, 81, 116, 117, 140
  as the Messiah, 43–44, 52, 58, 66, 72, 87, 101, 103, 115, 116, 127–28, 134, 163n
  not God, 15–16, 52, 111–12, 116, 145, 164
  parables, xviii, 19, 157–58
  prayer to, 6–7
  saving power, 2, 36, 46–47, 57–58, 91–92, 99, 134
  as Torah-observant, 31, 35
Jewish soul 42, 48
  leap to do God's will, 49–50
  lose your Jewish soul, 53–54
  mission and purpose, 48–50

Index of Subjects

not lose your Jewish soul, 43, 53
unique and chosen, 42–43, 48–50, 55, 56, 98

Jews
acceptance of MJ, xvii, 45–47, 115
conflict with MJ, xviin, 1–2, 51–53, 115, 163, 163n
in covenant relationship, 8–9, 11, 25, 53, 58, 70, 79, 81–82, 104, 134, 156
the elect, 38, 42, 48–49, 61–62, 64, 88, 89, 98–99, 135, 136
equality and inequality with Christians, 8, 39, 54–55, 61–62, 127, 130
evangelistic mission to, 3, 8, 38, 56, 107–08, 109, 116, 163n
historical neglect of, 38–39
identity, 2, 8, 38, 40–41, 49, 54, 62, 68, 79, 98, 115, 121, 143, 154
incomplete and completed, 2, 11, 38, 54–55, 60, 114, 127, 129–30
messianic idea, 45, 52, 128–29
in MJ, 9, 37, 42, 51, 58
opposed by Paul, 29–30, 63, 72, 81–82, 89, 100, 103–04, 143
for perpetuity, 31, 33, 36, 47, 93, 94, 96
reading the New Testament, 22, 132
rejected Jesus, 18, 39, 58, 69, 72, 89, 90–91
Talmudic, 39–42, 52, 94, 115, 128, 165
the traditional Jewish community, xvi–xvii, 2, 23, 51–53, 85, 114, 115
unsaved, 2, 18, 34, 54–55, 91–92, 96, 135

Judaism, 1, 38, 62, 79
defined, 51–53
MJ as a branch of, 14, 24, 28, 37, 41, 45
MJ not a branch of, xvi, xviin, xviii, 10, 56, 103, 112, 165
Paul's critique of, 30, 62, 63, 64, 76–77, 87
popular history of, 38–39
religion of, 45–46
Talmudic, 39–42

Kingdom of David, 11, 160–61
Kingdom of God, 4, 9, 107

Messianic Jews
affirm Judaism, 8, 38, 54, 61–64, 87, 108, 121
against Judaism, xviin, 18, 47, 52, 89, 155
apart from the church, 155, 164
Biblical interpretation, 22–23, 44–45, 75–76, 116–17, 143–46
of both Jewish and Christian beliefs, 12, 31, 33, 37, 45, 75–76 88, 93, 94, 105, 110–11, 114, 131, 143, 156
diversity within xvi–xvii, xviin, 14, 110
double movement to faith, 58–59, 113
embrace Jewishness, xviin, 2, 53–54, 58–59, 114, 135
heavenly vision 27, 31, 34–36
identity, 1–2, 13–14, 24, 43, 46–47, 50, 52, 58–59, 117, 155–56, 164–65
minority within, xv, xvi, 13, 16, 18, 132–33, 164–65
nothing new to offer, 41
not lose your soul, 43, 51
not Talmudic, 41, 43
post-supersessionist, 20
reestablishment, restoration, 11, 160–61
renewed (new) covenant, 58, 70, 113, 150, 156, 158
as scandal, xiv, 51–53
something new, 2, 10–11, 20, 26, 31, 126, 133
supersedes the church, 4, 4n, 24, 113, 130
supersedes Israel, 4, 113, 130, 155
Torah observant, 18n, 29, 33, 35–36, 47, 110, 114, 115, 136, 140, 145–46, 155
as true religion, xiv, 112, 130, 158

Index of Subjects

Messianic movement, xv–xvi, xvin, xvii, 2, 4, 4n, 13–14, 16, 18–19, 18n, 26, 37, 51, 55–56, 108, 160–65
Mt. Sinai (Mt. Horeb), 53, 68, 119, 121, 122–23, 124
Monotheism, xv, 15–16, 22, 44, 111–12, 117, 132, 141
   abandoned, xvin
   prayer, 6–7

New Testament, 7, 18, 35, 41, 99, 132, 143
   combine with Torah and Hebrew Bible 41, 45
   MJ use of xvii, 3, 23, 28, 112–13, 116–17
   post-supersessionist reading of, 20
   read monotheistically xv, xviii, 22, 44, 117, 132, 141
   read with Messianic paradigm, 22–23, 111–12, 144–46
   renaming, 26, 113, 147–49, 156–57
   revealing a messiah and the Messiah 37, 44, 116–17
   study of, 19, 117
   supersede the Old Testament, 20, 22, 23, 41, 44

Old Testament (Tanakh, Hebrew Bible), 5, 7, 34, 40, 44, 104
   co-opted by Christians, 7, 11, 20–22, 23, 26, 44, 143
   infallible to Orthodox Jews, 17
   misuse by Paul, 69, 73–74, 75–76, 80–81, 82, 83–84
   renaming, 26, 147–49
   Ten Commandments, 152, 155

Passover 23, 33, 108, 114, 119
Prophecy
   Biblical, 3, 32–36, 127, 128, 163n
   Word of, 5–6, 10–11, 160–62

Soteriology
   ark of salvation, 19
   Christian, 22, 100, 134, 136
   Dual covenants, 44, 105, 106–08, 114
   of MJ xiv, xvi, 17, 61, 63, 101–03, 105, 164–65
   in a parable, 46–47
   Pauline, 86, 88, 91–92

Temple, 31–36, 148–49
Third religion, xviii, 14, 28, 41, 62, 107, 113–16, 131, 162, 164
   third way, xvi, 10, 75, 94, 103, 105,
Torah, 26, 31, 68, 76, 78, 81, 99, 121, 123–24, 145, 156, 163n–64n
   the incarnation of, 29, 31, 116, 139, 144, 145
   Messianic observance, 18n, 35–36, 47, 78, 105, 114, 115, 140
   Oral and Written, 40–41
   teach, 9, 40
   Torah observance, 29–30, 33, 86, 101, 111, 122, 125, 136, 155
Transfiguration, 137–38
Trinity, xv, 7, 15, 18, 29, 44, 111, 144, 164
Two-offspring paradigm, 113–14

Vision on the road to Damascus, 31, 68, 75, 81–82, 90, 92, 100, 105, 116, 137–38

Index of Scripture

Genesis
17	142
17:21	68
21:12	44

Exodus
3:6	121
3:6–8	25
3:6–9	25
3:7–9	119
4:21	86
6:2–8	25
13:7–17:16	118
14:10–12	122
14:12	119
15–17	122
15:22–24	122
15:24	122
16:2–3	122
17:1–4	122
18	154
18:1–20:23	150
18:9	153
18:10	153
18:11	153
19	154
19:4	154
19:5	154
19:5–6	154
20:20	151

Leviticus
1:1–5:26	97
1:1–9	98
1:4	98

Numbers
7:89	144
11	122
11:1	123
11:1–3	122
11:4–9	123
11:31–33	123
14:1–2	123
14:10	123
14:12	123

Deuteronomy
6	25, 26
6:4	16, 26
6:20–25	25
6:25	26
28	142
29	87
29:4	87
32:21	84

1 Samuel
13:14	34

2 Samuel
1:16	104

Index of Scripture

1 Kings
2:33	104
19:18	85

2 Chronicles
26:16–21	34
36:23	6

Esther
3:1	47

Job
1:1	98
1:4–5	98
1:6	98

Psalms
23	44, 59
23:1	7
23:6	44
46:4–7	35
51	20–21, 22
51:11	22
121:1	7
121:4	12

Isaiah
8:14	75
28:14–22	76
28:15	76
28:16	75, 76, 80
28:22	76
45:1	44
45:1–8	129
60:3	145
65:1	83, 84
65:2	84

Ezekiel
40–48	31
40:1–4	31
44	32
44:15–16	33
45–46	35
45:16–46:18	27, 34
45:17	32
47	35
48	32
48:35	32

Daniel
9:25	44

Hosea
2:14–23	83

Joel
2	80
2:25–3:8	80
2:32	80, 81, 82

Malachi
1:1–2	69
4:6	5

Matthew
1:1	107
4:1–11	111
6:14	85
7:24–27	78
17:1–8	137
24	95
27:46	15

Mark
4: 26–29	xviii
9:1–8	137
13	95

Luke
9:28–36	137
16:1–13	157
16:6	157
16:8	158
16:9	158
16:12	158
16:13	158
21	95

John

1:1	116
1:1–4	144
1:1–18	44
3:2	10, 161
3:16	17
8:39	107
14:9–11	144
17:3	16, 111

Acts

2	22
2:22	112
2:24	111
9:1–9	31
9:18	90
11:15–18	56
14:19	30, 63
18:5–6	103–04
18:6	104
20:7	132
20:27	19n
22:4–16	31
26:9–18	31

Chapter 6 examines Romans 9, 10, and 11 in sequence and those verses are not indexed.

Romans

1–4	62
5–8	62
8–9	63
9–11	30, 62, 63
1:1	82
1:1–2	88
1:4	71
1:7	77
1:16	71
1:18	73
1:20	71
1:25	66
2:6	85
2:16	82
2:21	79
3:25	77
3:19–22	85
3:23	93
3:28–30	85
5:6	73
5:8	73
5:9	73
5:12	93
6:8	85
8:1	68
8:14	85
8:18–23	85
8:28	85
8:28–30	69
8:31	74
8:33	84
8:39	65
9:1–18	58
9:3	64
9:6	64
9:18	58
9:27	64
9:33	64
10:19	64
10:21	64
11	108
11:1	64
11:1–2	108
11:5	64
11:7	64
11:7–8	61
11:11	96
11:14	108
11:15	108
11:16–18	64
11:17	64
11:17–24	4n
11:21	64
11:24	108, 109
11:2	95, 96
11:26	61, 64, 96
11:28	108
11:29	108
11:31	108
11:32	100
11:36–12:1	63
12:1	94

Romans (continued)

13:10–12	92
13:11–12	85
15:13	85

1 Corinthians

1	60
1:3	112
1: 26–29	67
1:30	57, 58
2:14	17
15:20	96
15:20–23	137
15:22	68
15:51	95, 96
16:2	132

2 Corinthians

1:3	66
2:14–16	99
3:4–6	163n
3:11	66
4:4	17
5:17	44
5:19	44
11:24–26	30
11:26	30
5:20	83

Galatians

1:6–9	19n
1:8–9	29
2:21	30
3:10	29
3:21–26	85
3:29	68
4:4	128
4:28	68
5:12	30

Ephesians

2:2	17
2:14–15	143

Philippians

2:6–11	144

1 Thessalonians

2:15	103
2:15–16	143
4:15	92, 96

Titus

1:10–16	29
1:16	31

Hebrews

10	35
12:14	85

James

4:6	85

2 Peter

1:16–18	137

1 John

1:7	85
4:8	70
4:18	101

Revelation

3:12	16, 111

www.ingramcontent.com/pod-product-compliance
Lightning Source LLC
Chambersburg PA
CBHW062042220426
43662CB00010B/1614